Cuisine à la Carte

In the kitchens of the Dorchester Hotel, London, Anton Mosimann, left, puts the finishing touch to a seafood dish, with sous-chef John Hornsby.

Cuisine à la Carte

ANTON MOSIMANN

Introduction by
Quentin Crewe

MACMILLAN LONDON

First published 1981 by Northwood Books

Published 1983 by
PAPERMAC
a division of Macmillan Publishers Limited
4 Little Essex Street London WC2R 3LF
and Basingstoke

Associated companies in Auckland, Dallas, Delhi,
Dublin, Hong Kong, Johannesburg, Lagos, Manzini,
Melbourne, Nairobi, New York, Singapore, Tokyo,
Washington and Zaria

ISBN 0 333 35339 0

Black and white photographs and colour plates 1-4 by
David Montgomery. Colour plates 5-20 by John Lee.
Illustrations by Dick Barnard and Andrew Cloke.

A 'Catering Times' Book

Photosetting by Mallard Studios, Peterborough.
Printed in Hong Kong.

Contents

		Page
	List of Colour Plates	vii
	The Essential Mosimann — Introduction by Quentin Crewe	1
	Cooking Today	21
1	Basic Preparation	31
2	Sauces	63
3	Hors d'oeuvre	77
4	Soups	109
5	Egg Dishes	125
6	Fish Dishes	135
7	Shellfish Dishes	171
8	Meat Dishes	189
9	Poultry Dishes	223
10	Game Dishes	239
11	Vegetables	253
12	Sweets	267
	Glossary of Terms	294
	Index	297

Dedication

I would like to pay tribute to all those
who have supported and
encouraged me in this wonderful
profession. My sincere thanks, in
particular, to all my colleagues in
the Dorchester Hotel kitchen
brigade, especially John Hornsby,
Anton Edelmann and Mark Steeden
for their energetic help in the
preparation of this book. My thanks
are also due to Miles Quest, editor of
Catering Times, for his
encouragement and advice.

List of Colour Plates

Plate
Number

Facing
Page

PLATE 1   Discussing the merits of a batch of peaches for preserving. With Mosimann are sous-chef John Hornsby and the chef pâtissier François Cachia, right.   20

PLATE 2   The author tasting an unpasteurised Brie in the Dorchester kitchens with sous-chef Roy Raiman.   21

PLATE 3   Mosimann and his chefs examine lobsters and other seafood at Billingsgate fish market where, he says, 'You can really see what you're buying.'   36

PLATE 4   Anton Mosimann inspecting freshly-cooked crab at London's Billingsgate fish market.   37

PLATE 5   Méli-mélo de homard aux pointes d'asperges. Lobster salad with asparagus (Recipe 37).   100

PLATE 6   Above: Terrine Covent Garden. Vegetable terrine Covent Garden (Recipe 44).
Left: Rosette de saumon fumé au mousse de truite Dorchester. Smoked salmon with trout mousse Dorchester-style (Recipe 42).   101

PLATE 7   Above: Salade aux huîtres Catherine. Oyster salad with spinach (Recipe 40).
Left: Rendez-vous de fruits-de-mer à la crème de basilic. Seafood in basil sauce (Recipe 104).   116

PLATE 8   Billy Bye soup (Recipe 68).   117

PLATE 9   Above: Mousseline de coquilles St. Jacques. Mousseline of scallops with fresh tomato purée. (Recipe 57).
Left: Elixir de cailles aux oeufs. Clear quail soup with soft eggs. (Recipe 61).   164

PLATE 10   Filet de rouget à la vapeur sous cloche. Fillets of red mullet with vinaigrette sauce (Recipe 99).   165

PLATE 11   Above: Tronçon de turbot soufflé aux écrevisses. Turbot soufflé with crayfish (Recipe 87).
Left: Coquilles St. Jacques Galloises. Scallops fried in butter with leeks (Recipe 56).   180

PLATE 12   Mignons de boeuf aux échallotes. Mignons of beef with red wine sauce and chopped shallots (Recipe 120).   181

PLATE 13   Côte de boeuf marinée aux herbes du jardin. Grilled rib of beef with herbs and butter sauce (Recipe 121).   212

PLATE 14   Foie de veau vénitienne. Calves' liver with onions and Madeira sauce (Recipe 139).   213

PLATE 15   Màgret de canard grillé—Nossi-Bé. Grilled duck's breast with green peppercorns (Recipe 153).   228

PLATE 16   Poussin aux légumes grillés. Grilled baby chicken with grilled vegetables (Recipe 149).   229

PLATE 17   Compôte de fruits et coulis de framboises. Preserved fruits and raspberry sauce (Recipes 175 to 177 and 183).   276

PLATE 18   Above: Assiette des sorbets Christine. Plate of assorted sorbets (Recipe 200).
Right: Feuilleté aux framboises Eileen Atkins. Raspberries in puff pastry (Recipe 182).   277

PLATE 19   Above: Soufflé aux fruits de la passion. Passion fruit soufflé (Recipe 180).   292

PLATE 20   Above: Crêpe sans rival. Pancake with a cream and fruit filling (Recipe 190).
Left: Ananas au poivre Jean et Paul. Peppered pineapple with sauce of crème de Cacao (Recipe 181).   293

Mosimann, always eager to communicate his knowledge and skill, vastly enjoys entertaining visitors. Quentin Crewe, author and food writer, visited the Dorchester many times before writing this profile.

The essential Mosimann

Foreword by

Quentin Crewe

What most human beings seem to find so hard to achieve is a balance between the contradictory aspects of their natures. If they are generous they are feckless, if they are hardworking they are humourless, if they are witty they are cruel, if they are kindly they are wet. Few people are shrewdly generous, funny and industrious and so on.

The mind, said Rémy de Gourmand, should be like an hotel — capable of entertaining several contradictory ideas at the same time. It is a matter of balance.

Anton Mosimann, like the hotels he has worked in all his life, manages to balance the disparate traits of his nature in such a way as to preserve an elegant harmony.

His most striking characteristic is certainty. In most people this would lead, even in success, to dogmatism, brashness, severity, smugness, ruthlessness and a good few other insupportable vices. Mr. Mosimann balances his certainty with modesty, courtesy, humour, kindliness and an external eagerness to learn — thereby making his certainty a reality and reaching the peak of his profession at the age of twenty-nine.

Anton Mosimann was born at Solothurn in Switzerland in 1947. He was the only child of his parents, who had a combined family restaurant and farm. They left Solothurn when Anton was five and bought what he describes as a good, bourgeois restaurant at Nidau.

For the next ten years the restaurant itself was Anton's home. The Mosimanns had no living room apart from the restaurant and it was at one of the tables that the boy used to do his homework. It did not matter to him because, by the time he was six, he was certain about what he wanted to do. He wanted to be a chef.

On one day a week the restaurant was shut. Anton's parents would go off for the day, but by the time he was eight the small boy would stay behind and invite his friends to dinner. Not his school pals, but grown-up friends of twenty-five or thirty. It became quite an honour in the town to be asked by little Anton to come to eat his spaghetti bolognese or Wurstsalat or cheese fondue.

When he was twelve, he decided he would need a car when he was eighteen. He collected broken electric light bulbs and sold the metal. He gathered quantities of newspapers and sold them. He traded in bicycles, worked in other restaurants and cooked in the family one if his father was playing cards. He got his car.

It was a slightly desolate life for a young boy and he is conscious that something was missing. With his own children, he will see that things are different. Nevertheless, they were a happy family in their way and there was always an awareness of other people's lesser fortune. The restaurant was open at Christmas and the Mosimanns invited all the lonely people of the neighbourhood to come to eat for nothing.

If his childhood was somewhat austere, it was nothing compared with what was to come. From the very first the pattern was set — a strange mixture of good fortune and his own plan for his life. Looking at it with hindsight, one can understand what Julius Caesar meant when he said, 'All good generals are lucky.' It is a question of positioning oneself correctly for any luck that may be going.

How many young aspirants, who have to plead to be taken on, might think Anton was lucky, at fifteen, to be *asked* to be an apprentice! But would he have been asked had he not cooked for his friends when he was eight?

Whatever the case, he went off to the Hotel Baeren in Twann at the management's invitation. 'There I learned not finesse, but how to work.' He used to start at 8 a.m. and never finished earlier than 11 p.m., with only one hour's break during the day. He had one day off each week, but had to use it to do eight hours'

Breakfast in the chef's dining room after a dawn visit to Billingsgate fish market; as usual, Mosimann is keen to make a point, using such visits as a teaching opportunity for the younger chefs and commis.

*A final inspection
before service.*

schooling. He was so tired and lonely that at night he would go to bed crying.

But it meant that, at little more than seventeen, he won, as the best student, his *Diplômé de Cuisinier* — which is normally taken at nineteen. From that time on, Anton was always the youngest.

He had already planned his next move well in advance. He had written to Henri Dessibourg at the Palace Hotel at Villars and there he got his first job in the winter of 1964.

'It was run like a military operation, but after the Baeren I thought I was on holiday.' Even so, it was his first experience of the meaning of perfection in cuisine. 'Each piece of potato, with eight of us cutting them up, had to be exactly the same size. No more than ten per cent off was allowed for wastage.' The *pommes risolées* had to be golden. If they were brown, they were sent back. Besides perfection, he learnt that a head chef must be fair but hard. The régime was extremely strict and old-fashioned. All the cooks had to wear their hats at lunch and their post was never given to them until 3 p.m., after the service.

The next summer he spent in Rome at the Cavalieri Hilton, where the chef, René Rastello, used to thump the table so hard that once he broke his own finger. The next winter he was back in Switzerland at Sils-Maria, in the Waldhaus, where he was *commis saucier*, though he still found time to do courses on diet and *flambé* work.

There followed three years in Canada, including being *sous-chef* at the Canadian Pavilion at Expo 67. He managed to do a How-to-teach course as well. At twenty-one, he already had his own flat with a sauna and swimming pool. He was offered several senior jobs, but he turned them down.

Anton was not ready. Back he went to Switzerland, learning various aspects of his trade, including working in St. Moritz under Monsieur Defrance, who had himself worked under Escoffier. The old man was by then eighty-seven and rather eccentric, falling asleep over the stoves, inclined to pinching the knives of his underlings and selling them and drinking at least one bottle of champagne a day.

In 1970, Anton applied for a post as *sous-chef* at the Swiss Pavilion for Expo 70 in Osaka. To his surprise, he was given the job of Head Chef with thirty-five chefs under him, twenty-five Japanese. The luck was holding, you might say, but it was he who won the gold medal at the Fair. And on the plane to Osaka, he met the head housekeeper for the Pavilion — Kathrin — and he fell in love.

Yet if the luck was there, the plan was not complete. Anton was still not ready. Not ready to take the offers of Head Chef at the Tokyo Hilton, the Singapore something or other; not ready, either to marry Kathrin — not until he had his *Chef de Cuisine Diplômé*, the highest Swiss culinary award.

So it was back to Switzerland for nearly five years as a *chef de partie* in five different Palace Hotels while he added to his knowledge.

Of course, he got his *Chef de Cuisine Diplômé* — the youngest chef ever to do so — and Anton married Kathrin on Friday 13th April 1973. In 1974 he decided that his experience in *pâtisserie* was not great enough. He spent the winter at the Palace Hotel in Gstaad, as a *commis pâtissier,* the humblest of rôles — 'I was most pleased' he says. It was there that the Dorchester Hotel sought him out and offered him the job of first *Sous-chef,* with a view to his taking over the kitchens of this famous hotel from Eugene Käufeler, who had ruled over them for twenty-five years — indeed since Anton was three. A year later he did just that. In November 1976, when he was still only twenty-nine, Anton Mosimann became *Maître-Chef des Cuisines* at the Dorchester.

Ever since he was fifteen, Anton had always known that he would one day be the head chef of a large hotel kitchen. That was his plan. Every time he moved it was because he chose to work under a particular chef, from whom he could learn a particular skill. That was his certainty.

Such determination, sureness of touch and steadiness of purpose, we feel instinctively must be coupled with self-absorption, crude ambition and a ruthless disregard for others.

When you first meet Anton you could, at a pinch, imagine his having these driving characteristics. His manner is a little precise and formal. His English, while almost perfect, has a flicker of Hollywood German Officer about it. He seems to be an onlooker rather than a participant; his reactions a little studied, even calculated. You wonder whether he is laughing at your joke because he thinks it funny or because it is polite to laugh at jokes.

How to find out? His friends say that, while he is a most agreeable companion, they never see him let his hair down. He is always the same — reserved, proper, exquisitely polite. His wife, Kathrin, is equally correct.

Neither of them drinks much. The formalities are carefully preserved and their way of life is somewhat old-fashioned. They do not even have a television set in their flat in Ennismore Gardens. Anton is an excellent father to their two sons, Philipp who is five and Mark who is three. Their family life is perhaps particularly private — possibly the more so because of Anton's memory of his own rather detached childhood.

The only way to find an answer is to watch him work. A chef, after all, has little life apart from his work and any clues to his nature must lie in his work.

On one of the first few days after Anton arrived at the Dorchester, he heard an announcement over the Tannoy: 'Is there anyone working here called Paul Carter? If so, he's wanted on the telephone.' He was horrified. Did they really not know who was working in the place? Was the staff really so unimportant?

Today, when he arrives in the kitchens at 8.30 a.m.,

A head chef has to work in close touch with the front of house staff. John Curry, manager of the Dorchester's Grill Room has been with the hotel for 15 years which makes Mosimann a comparative newcomer — but their relationship is a happy one.

after a brisk walk across the park, his first act is to say good morning to as many of the eighty-five or so people who work under him as possible — shaking them by the hand and calling them by name. It may sound a trifle disingenuous, until you see him put his arm round the deaf and dumb boy, Sam, who helps unload and check the produce as it arrives. Then you recognise this ritual as a genuine human gesture.

After an hour of preliminary checking, the first of dozens of trips round the huge kitchens, there is a meeting with the *chefs de partie*. They crowd into Anton's little dining room, about ten feet square with an oval table and half a dozen too large red leather chairs. The meeting starts with a discussion of the previous day's events. Anton passes on any comments the customers may have made and thanks everyone for his share in any successes.

He has already planned the day's menu with the Chef's Clerk who has checked with the *chef garde-manger* what is available. He reads them out. The pantry man points out that he has some pigeons which are ready to use that day.

Anton then gives out any other news of importance. He shows them some newly printed menus, mentions the matter of their new contracts, says it is all right for a team to go to the Culinary Exhibition in Frankfurt, reads out a postcard from a colleague who has left to work in the West Indies, and raises the matter of raffle tickets for the staff dance, which his secretary Hilary has to sell. The *chef pâtissier* says he has five thousand peaches ready for bottling. Can he borrow two people to help?

It is all over in twenty minutes, but everyone goes away knowing that Anton is aware of what he is doing, feeling in touch with the customer and realising he is part of a team.

Every Tuesday, when the points arising from the meeting have been settled, Anton immediately has another meeting to look at the menus for functions already arranged for a week ahead. This is held with the first *sous-chef*, Mr. Roy Raiman, the *sous-chef* Mr.

With the Dorchester's cellar manager Stephen Price (left) and Luigi
Averoni, head wine waiter of the Grill Room, Mosimann discusses
the merits of a particular wine for a special dinner.

A prime forerib of Scotch beef — the Dorchester can use up to 35 ribs a week. Mosimann is convinced that it is the best of each season's produce that determines the standard of any cuisine.

Brian Howitt and the *chef pâtissier*, Mr. Cachia. Mr. Howitt has been at the Dorchester for forty-two years, Mr. Raiman more than thirty, Mr. Cachia twenty. Anton addresses all of them as Mr. Brian, Mr. Roy and so on, as a mark of respect. This meeting is to ensure that they have time to buy the best produce for each occasion.

'Next week, so far, we have a cocktail party on Monday. We will need canapés for two hundred. On Wednesday we have a lunch for two hundred and fifty. We will have a choice of three starters — oysters, smoked salmon and hors d'oeuvre.'

They agree to order enough oysters for about half the people, smoked salmon for the other half and to prepare about twelve hors d'oeuvre. They know from experience that this is roughly the proportion in which the guests will choose.

'We have a special dinner for four covers, including a *sorbet de menthe*; can you make sure we have some fresh leaves of mint?'

'On Thursday we have a lunch for four hundred and fifty. Please order *filets mignons*. It is a Foyles lunch. We must consider the elderly — not too heavy, not too strange.'

Mr. Brian proposes broccoli as a vegetable, if it is available. Anton accepts the suggestion, as if it were a wholly new idea — not patronisingly, but pleased that Mr. Brian should be sufficiently involved.

'On Friday we have an Embassy lunch — no pork, no ham. We will need special beef chipolatas.'

Anton is immensely strict about observing the religious scruples of the customers. He would not dream of allowing even a spoonful of stock with a ham-bone in it to be used for a Muslim or Jewish customer. A whole new stock will have to be made

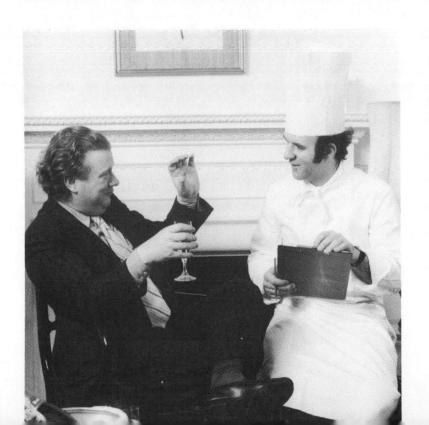

'Can we have it cooked the way you did it last month?' asks gourmet Alistair McAlpine, discussing a forthcoming private dinner.

A banquet — one of many for the Dorchester is an important banqueting hotel in London. Extra hands are called in to fold 250 chicken breasts stuffed with mango. Mosimann, ever the perfectionist, explains how he wants it done.

even if one person orders a minestrone in his room. In any sauce he will substitute lemon juice for white wine.

That done, Anton moves next door to his office and with his secretary goes through his correspondence, deals with general administration, considers thoughtfully the two or three applications he gets each day for jobs.

Mr. Watson, the food and beverage manager, pops in with an urgent request for suggested menus for an E.M.I. lunch for a hundred and twenty people.

'Shall I give them standard ones?' asks Mr. Watson, doubtfully.

'Oh, no,' says Anton. 'What sort of an occasion is it?'

Mr. Watson elaborates. The Chef thinks for a little . . . then he rattles off three complete menus — two with three courses, one with four, all at the same price.

What goes through his mind while he thinks? 'The colour of the menu, the texture of it, the ease for the waiters for the number of people to be served. It is fun.' Suddenly one realises that every minute of the last two hours, into which he has packed as much as many people do in a day, has been fun — not just for him, but for everyone.

Now it is time to go out into the kitchens again for another tour. Sam has just unloaded some lamb — a saddle. Anton picks it up, sniffs it. 'Look at the "eye", so little fat, it is beautiful. You hold it. Isn't it lovely?' I often wonder what an outsider would make of a chef's enthusiasm for a piece of meat, a side of smoked salmon, a box of vegetables. It is the knowledge which is fascinating, then his happiness at what he knows he can make of it.

Round the kitchen he goes. 'Clean that.' His eye is ever watchful. An apprentice is missing a button. He is asked to get it put on. Another has not tied his neckerchief properly. Twenty minutes later we meet the buttonless boy again. Still no button. Told, with a snap, to get it done at once.

Pause by the fish. Anton glows over the scallops, squeezes a drop of lemon on one to show it is still alive.

Each decapitated egg is given its regulation amount of special dressing — no more, no less.

Decides then to give them to some guests he has coming for lunch in his special dining room. Then he falls in love with a haddock. Orders that too. 'Too fishy,' he says. 'Never mind, no one can choose between two such beautiful things and we must have the lamb. Anyhow it is just friends.'

That may not seem the height of devil-may-care, but it is a chink.

A word with Mr. Frank Finlay, in the bakery which turns out sixteen thousand rolls a day. Into the *pâtisserie*, where the five thousand peaches are being bottled by girls in gloves. Anton peers into the fridge and tells the *commis* to take out the *pâtisseries* which will be used for today's lunch. The watchful eye again. Over to Ernie Callard, who is performing amazing financial calculations.

'Do you know, when I came, he had been twenty-five years as *chef rôtisseur*? He needed a change and had this untapped talent. Now he does the most wonderful job.'

It was one of Anton's major re-organisations, moving people to the right place. 'That and motivation.'

Twelve o'clock. Time to be in the upstairs kitchens, before lunch starts in the restaurant. And there you lose him. He darts about, tasting, checking, advising, commanding, rescuing. (In Japan at Expo 70, the mayonnaise came out too thick. Only Anton suddenly realised the eggs were bigger.) Anyhow, it is no good following him there, because it is the ultimate exercise of his art, learned over thirty years, starting at his mother's simple farmhouse stove.

There, except when he has guests for lunch (and even then as often as not), he cooks until 2.30 p.m. Every day he cooks for at least three hours, often five or six.

At three o'clock he goes home for a couple of hours with his family. Then he is back, repeating all the preparation and work for the evening service. He is lucky to be home by 11 p.m.

But that is not always all of his day. At least twice a month he goes to one of the markets — to Billingsgate, or New Covent Garden. For Anton, they are a delight. He believes that the London markets have some of the best produce in the world. 'It is hard work not to make something good out of it.' Produce is for him a source of inspiration. 'In the market I once saw some scallops and, when I got back, some wonderful leeks had just arrived. I went straight off and made a new dish combining the two — but I might never have thought of it without the sight of them'.

He could hardly believe, when he was in Los Angeles, that the hotel chefs there never bought the beautiful fresh pineapples grown in California. 'They used tinned ones — when the markets were full of real ones. In America, cost is all that counts. Naturally, we work to a reasonable overall percentage, but cost is never a dominating consideration.'

Another part of Anton's time may be taken up with preparations for culinary competitions. He likes to take two or three of his chefs off to any serious competition that is going. In his time he has won more than thirty gold medals in different parts of the world. The object is not vainglory.

He sees these awards as objectives for his staff — who otherwise cook somewhat in limbo, necessarily removed from the customer. They give him opportunities for teaching, for showing what others are doing, for promoting a team spirit.

Furthermore he goes off himself at least once a year to learn from others, to work in the kitchens of one of the great French Chefs — Paul Bocuse, Michel Guérard, the Troisgros brothers. It is an everlasting quest.

So from his work and his way of working, we get a new light on the character of Anton Mosimann. The certainty is there all right, but it is balanced by dedication, not self-absorption; by a desire always to improve on what has gone before, not by crude ambition. By a wholly generous recognition of what others contribute to his achievements, a wish to share that success and almost a compulsion to communicate his knowledge and his skill to his younger colleagues.

But still there is something missing. Is there not in his eye a spark of merriment which one, perhaps, ignored at the beginning?

The answer to that lies in the food he produces. Naturally, at the Dorchester there has to be the old stand-by food of the grand hotel. This he produces, giving it incidentally a freshness which makes one wonder whether we were right ever to get bored with it. (For a whimsical friend of mine he recently produced a steamed pudding which was the lightest miracle you could imagine.) Then, again, he belongs to the school

With sous-chef Roy Raiman, who has been at the Dorchester for over
30 years, Mosimann conducts an informal inspection of the cheese
board before service. Patriotically, his favourite cheese is Emmental
from Switzerland.

A commis gets a quick
tutorial on preparing a
sauce.

of the so-called *nouvelle cuisine*. 'Smaller portions, more selection, fresher ingredients,' is how he describes it. But each truly great chef has his own distinctive touch over and above the sheer skill, his own genius beyond the superb artistry.

In Anton Mosimann's case, the surprising thing is that this extra, individual touch is an almost rash sense of adventure. As you wander through the recipes which compose this book, you will be constantly surprised. Can you do *that* with a brussels sprout? Can you put those things together?

Like all chefs Anton believes that 'happiness is seeing a hundred and twenty people made happy.' It is

a gift to give. For him part of happiness is surprise. He devised for the Dorchester the *menu surprise*, a set meal, at a set price which varies every day and which may consist of anything.

Anton's manner may seem old-fashioned, but then, for all the talk of modern cooking, his is an old-fashioned profession. Yet, in fact, he performs amazing tricks. Foie gras with a purée of bananas and walnuts. Soup covered with gold leaf. Soufflé with Passion Fruit. Blue salt with his Huîtres au Champagne Moscovite. The unexpected mixture, the intriguing pattern, the startling visual effect — those are the hallmarks which he puts upon the basic exactitude of his immeasurably fine cuisine. Witty often, adventurous always and even risky.

And so it is with his nature. Seemingly staid, apparently unbendingly correct. Until one day you make a joke, even a criticism. And instead of wondering when he laughs, you know from the quality of his laughter that you have a friend.

Quentin Crewe

PLATE 1
Discussing the merits of a batch of peaches for preserving. With Mosimann are sous-chef John Hornsby and the chef pâtissier François Cachia, right.

PLATE 2
The author tasting an unpasteurised Brie in the Dorchester kitchens with sous-chef Roy Raiman.

Cooking today

The good cook loves and enjoys his work and all good cooks have in common both the desire and the capacity to produce something really first-rate. There has never been a more exciting time to be a cook and to appreciate to the full all the marvellous produce that is nowadays at our disposal.

As an art, a science and a skill, cooking has developed and improved in parallel with society itself. Greater prosperity, increasingly sophisticated tastes — and sufficient leisure to enjoy them — the spread of overseas travel: all these have contributed to our appreciation of food and wine. More than that, modern transportation in its widest sense has ensured that wherever you are it is possible to find the finest fresh produce, the raw materials which form the basis of the cook's repertoire.

It is this produce — the best of each season's vegetables, meat and fish — which determines the cook's individual dishes and the menu as a whole. I believe wholeheartedly that the cook must spend time, daily if at all possible, to examine the fresh produce on offer and to buy accordingly.

Time after time I find, when wandering through the markets with their enormous, attractive displays, that they stimulate me to create and compose.

I see the fresh coquilles St. Jacques already in the frying pan, together with the aromatic fresh basil, and I know that just fifteen seconds in sizzling butter will transform them into a seafood delicacy, nestling on a bed of freshly puréed young leeks, to tempt the most blasé of palates.

I like to see all the lovely, fresh colourful vegetables ready to be boiled. Their different shapes, colours, textures, inspired me to create from them a lovely

Aiming for perfection means constant checking and testing. Mosimann tries to inspect as much as possible before service. "A really good cuisine", he says "demands a single-minded, almost holy, devotion".

terrine, which I christened Terrine Covent Garden in honour of the market.

Strolling around Billingsgate before the sunrise, I gaze upon the fresh turbot, halibut, sole and seafood, and I cannot wait to get back to the kitchen and produce a dish that will do justice to their freshness, aromas and textures.

Visiting the markets has, too, a more pragmatic advantage; one sees what one buys. Ordering by telephone deprives the cook of this essential factor.

Nevertheless, the purchase of even the best raw materials is not enough. The cook must also observe the following points:

• A really good cuisine demands a single-minded, almost holy devotion. Success depends on perfection in the smallest details.

- He tries, tastes, samples and tries again, like a composer searching out his theme on the keyboard and elaborating on it.
- The artistic arrangement and presentation of dishes is essential. But . . . complication is the enemy of good cooking; extravagant displays and elaborate garnishes should be avoided.
- Sauces should be the perfectly harmonious accompaniment of the individual dishes. A supreme cook is recognised by his sauces.

I have found it absolutely necessary to refine traditional cuisine again and again, to create a lighter, more natural result. One of the essential factors here is to pay more attention than hitherto to the rate and length of the cooking process.

For instance, apart from the vegetable purées, most green vegetables (particularly French beans, mange-tout, asparagus etc.) should be prepared according to the ancient and proven Asiatic tradition; in other words, they should be 'crunchy'. If vegetables are soft and overcooked they have lost their flavour and their shape as well as their natural colour and vitamins. In exactly the same way, fish should be steamed, poached, grilled or fried — most accurately to the right point.

What is Cooking?

Reduced to absolute basics, 'cooking' encompasses all the various methods and techniques of preparing the raw materials of food into good, appetising dishes.

In order to practise cooking successfully, the cook should be not only enthusiastic, dedicated and creative; he should be familiar, too, with its scientific, culinary and practical principles and methods. Without turning himself into a quasi-scientist, the chef must nevertheless be aware of why food acts and reacts in the ways it does — in other words, of the basic elements of the culinary art.

- Biology: the study of the nature and properties of foodstuffs. Cooking is easier if you understand the basic elements, such as, quite simply, *why* milk boils over. Or why salt is important, not only as a seasoning, but also to conserve and keep the chlorophyll in the leaves of green vegetables.

- Economy: the study of the origin of foodstuffs, their transport and trade.
- Physiology: the digestive process and the sense of taste; the effect of nutrition on healthy and sick people.
- Psychology: determination of the psychological effects of good and bad nutrition on individuals and on people in general.
- Administration and man-management: the professional cook these days is likely to find himself in charge of a large kitchen. Without the ability to administer such a kitchen and to get the best out of his team, his creative skills as a chef may be wasted.
- Aesthetics: cultivation of a sense of beauty, development of a feeling for the proper shapes and colours in good cuisine, and of their influence on the selection, preparation and presentation of food.

The good cook is an eternal apprentice. He is prepared to travel far and wide, not only in his own country, but to as many lands as he can visit, professionally and at his leisure. I have had the good fortune to work in eight different countries, and the opportunity to collect ideas and inspiration as well as knowledge, in all of them. Such travel allows one not only to get to know the various countries and their people, but also to learn their eating habits and the origins of these.

Thus, whoever wishes to master the art of cookery must be thoroughly familar with its theory and practice. An excellent knowledge of food products, good sense of smell and taste, and creative talent are its most important requirements. But the cook must, too, have a link with the ultimate 'patron' of his art — the customer. People nowadays are increasingly willing and eager to try new dishes; but it is vital that whoever is in direct contact with the customer is a good salesman who believes in the chef's work.

Very often I have the chance to speak to customers myself, and can persuade them to try a different dish

At the chefs' morning meeting, the day's menus are discussed with senior staff — and fresh produce is critically examined.

from their first choice — if I sincerely believe they will enjoy my recommendations. At the same time, however original and creative your own special dishes may be, I do not believe in changing original 'farmland' or 'peasant' dishes such as, in this country, steak and kidney pudding, Irish stew and so on. The good cook knows when to innovate, when to improve — and when to leave well alone!

It is true, then, that the raw materials provided by nature are in themselves the most perfect victuals. But most of them require a process of preparation that differs according to their species and condition, and which varies according to different countries and their social mores. Retaining the original taste of these ingredients, however, is one of the most important principles of modern cookery. It is to that principle, above all others, that I dedicate this book.

The good cook should always remember the axiom of the great August Escoffier: '*La bonne cuisine est celle où les choses ont le goût de ce qu'elles sont.*'

Let us then take a look behind the scenes — at the day-to-day running of a great kitchen.

Six a.m. For some in the ever-demanding (but often rewarding) catering business it is the finish of a shift — for others the beginning. The kitchen, the nucleus of the hotel, provides a twenty-four hour round-the-clock service for the hotel's guests and visitors, which, as you can well imagine, requires extensive organisation. As *maître-chef des cuisines* of The Dorchester Hotel, my aim is to maintain and improve the standard of cuisine that Dorchester clientèle have come to expect, which is no mean task, and in fact would be nigh impossible without one hundred per cent support and teamwork from my eighty-strong kitchen brigade.

I am a firm believer in the necessity for staff motivation. My first prerogative each day is to have a little chat with every member of our brigade, always calling each by his Christian name and praising any culinary achievement where appropriate. I will never ask anybody to do anything that I could not (or would not) do myself. It is important that the right people are

in the right job for cooking demands so many qualities — concentration, a serious approach to work, mixed with considerable tact and understanding.

At our daily 9.30 a.m. meeting we discuss the work for the day, events of the previous day, and any other kitchen news.

We make trips to the fish, meat and fruit markets, and have been visited by such gastronomes as Paul Bocuse, Michel Guérard, the Troisgros brothers, and Roger Vergé, just to name a few. Many stimulating discussions always follow such visits, and help to show my brigade what a fascinating business we are involved in and how each day can hold new discoveries.

Two further courses of action I use to motivate our staff are the weekly training sessions which everybody is encouraged to attend, and the help I give to those who wish to work abroad to gain further experience. So far, we have arranged 'working holidays' in France, Switzerland, Belgium and Germany.

Entering culinary competitions and exhibitions is

An early-morning visit to Billingsgate, London's fish market, with some of his chefs. Mosimann finds the markets exciting, almost inspirational. It also has a more pragmatic advantage: 'One sees what one buys.'

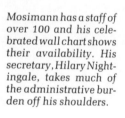

Mosimann has a staff of over 100 and his celebrated wall chart shows their availability. His secretary, Hilary Nightingale, takes much of the administrative burden off his shoulders.

another feature of life in our kitchens and a great way of stimulating interest, especially with our record of over thirty gold medals won in international competitions over the last five years, and also winning the England Final of the best 'commis rôtisseur' for the past four.

We maintain records of our V.I.P. guests' likes and whims, the knowledge of which I make sure is passed to the staff on duty. We pride ourselves upon our standards of cuisine, and we will always do our best to fulfil any request.

Such efficiency is only achieved with a first class administrative back-up. Recipe requests, staff to be interviewed, wage queries and press articles are only a small portion of the paperwork and office back-up to be dealt with each day. I like to spend as much time as possible actually working in the kitchen, so we have Hilary, my full time secretary, to deal with the paperwork. Another facet of our daily administration is our 'Mini Computer' — a wall chart into which coloured pegs are inserted to represent the progress of each chef, i.e. green pegs for sick leave, yellow for college days, and so on. I can therefore devote myself whole-heartedly to cooking and working with my staff, safe in the knowledge that we are sound in administrative matters.

Above all, one must never lose sight of the fact that our prime objective is a 'delighted', not just 'satisified' customer, which can only be achieved with first class organisation.

ANTON MOSIMANN

Chapter 1

Basic Preparation

Basic Preparation

The words "to cook" are often misused in the kitchen. There are only a few raw materials which are cooked. I always say "whoever is fully conversant with the basic methods of preparation has the whole world of cooking at his feet because these are the multiplication tables of cooking". Whether he is cooking in London, New York, Tokyo, Paris or Berne is of no importance. The basis always remains the same.

It is the understanding, command and correct use of the basic methods of preparation which allow for the perfect accomplishment of the cooking process. Whoever is able to do that is also in a position to produce the more complicated dishes.

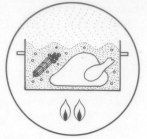

Blanching
Blanchir

A process by which food is brought rapidly to boiling point in water and boiled for a very short time. Rinse and plunge into cold water quickly (to prevent further cooking).
It is a process that often takes place as a preliminary to other cooking methods, for example boiling, sautéing or glazing.

Blanching (in water):

Potatoes: Place into deep boiling salted water. Bring to the boil. Remove potatoes quickly. Allow to cool on a tray preferably with a towel.

Vegetables: Place into rapidly boiling salted water (1:10). Bring to the boil again. Rinse quickly and plunge into cold water. Remove vegetables and use otherwise. This method guarantees that the chlorophyll-containing vitamins and mineral salts are retained in green vegetables.

Bones: Bring to the boil in cold water and cool under running water.

Chicken: Bring to the boil in cold water for white poultry stock.

Meat: Bring to the boil in cold water.

Note: Starting with cold water causes the cells to open, therefore there is a loss of taste. Starting with hot water causes the cells to close, therefore the taste is retained.

Blanching (in oil)
Blanching in hot oil is equivalent to a pre-frying process: e.g. fish, meat, vegetables, potatoes at approximately 130°C (250°F.) Leave to cool rapidly.

Poaching
Pocher

Poaching is a gentle and protective method of food preparation, which is carefully carried out in a liquid or in a container in a bain-marie at 65°-80°C (150°-175°F).
- Fish can be poached at 65°-80°C/150°-175°F with a little liquid.
- Fish can be poached in a court-bouillon (see recipe 7).
- Poultry can be poached in a white poultry stock (see recipe 1) after being blanched first.

In liquid: Fish, poultry, offal, eggs can be poached in a stock, bouillon or court-bouillon.
In bain-marie: Various fillings, stuffings, vegetables, custard and desserts can be poached in a container in a bain-marie.
Note: When the temperature of the poaching medium rises above 80°C/175°F, the protein of the food begins to break down.

Typical food	fish
	terrines
	poultry
	custard
Typical cooking equipment	stove, roasting or baking oven, rôtissoir sautoir

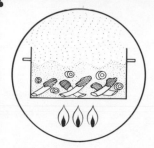

Simmering
Bouillir

Simmering is a method of preparation between poaching and boiling. Allow to simmer at a temperature between 95°-98°C/about 203°F.

Meat dishes: For boiled meat, lamb, veal, tongue, start off with hot salted water or stock, possibly blanching first. Bring to the boil and then allow to simmer. Do not cover.

Clear broths and aspic jelly: Start off with cold water or stock to extract the flavour. To obtain a clear broth and to avoid the breakdown of protein, the casserole should never be covered.

Heat transference agent	water or stock
Method of heat transference	convection
Working temperature	up to 98°C/210°F
Typical food	meat
	stocks
	broths
Typical cooking equipment	stove
	gas ring
	marmite

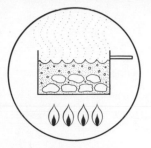

Boiling
Cuire

To cook in boiling water or stock up to the required tenderness (or until the food is tender). It is mainly used for pasta, rice and dry vegetables.
Potatoes and root vegetables should be started off in cold salted water and covered.
Green vegetables should be started off in a little salted boiling water and preferably left to boil with the lid on.
Pasta should be started off in hot salted water with a little oil and left uncovered, cooking rapidly. Pasta must be cooked *al dente* in a proportion of 1:10 to the water.

Heat transference agent	water
Method of heat transference	convection
Working temperature	100°C/212°F
Typical food	pasta
	rice
	potatoes
	vegetables
	soup
Typical cooking equipment	stove
	gas ring
	marmite

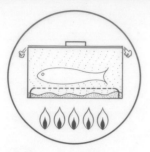

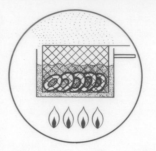

Steaming
Cuire à la vapeur

This method of preparation is being used more and more frequently. To retain the original taste there is no better method than steaming because it is very quick and is particularly suitable for fish, crustaceans, meat, poultry, vegetables, potatoes, cereals, desserts, etc.

Without pressure:
Use a heavy container with a perforated base, grating or basket and a heavy cover. Keep boiling water at level beneath the food — Replace water lost by evaporation.

Under pressure:
Wet steam: In pressure cookers.
Dry steam: In high speed steam cookers.
With this method, however, it is particularly important to ensure that only the very freshest of raw materials are used.

Heat transference agent	steam
Method of heat transference	convection condensation
Working temperature	200°-220°C 400°-425°F
Typical food	potatoes fish vegetables rice etc.
Typical cooking equipment	steam pressure pot automatic high pressure steamer

Deep fat frying
Frire

To prepare by immersing food in oil or fat.
It is advisable to blanch the food first and then deep fry until crisp at approximately 140°-190°C/ about 340°F. Suitable for fish, meat, poultry, vegetables, potatoes, sweets.
It is important that the temperature of the fat is not suddenly lowered during cooking, otherwise the food will absorb too much fat.
Potato dishes such as chips, pommes gaufrettes, dauphin, should not be blanched.

Heat transference agent	fat, oil
Method of heat transference	convection
Working temperature	140°-190°C/ 275°-375°F
Typical food	chips meat and pieces of meat doughnuts etc. vegetables
Typical cooking equipment	friteuse

PLATE 3
Mosimann and his chefs examine lobsters and other seafood at Billingsgate fish market where, he says, 'You can really see what you're buying.'

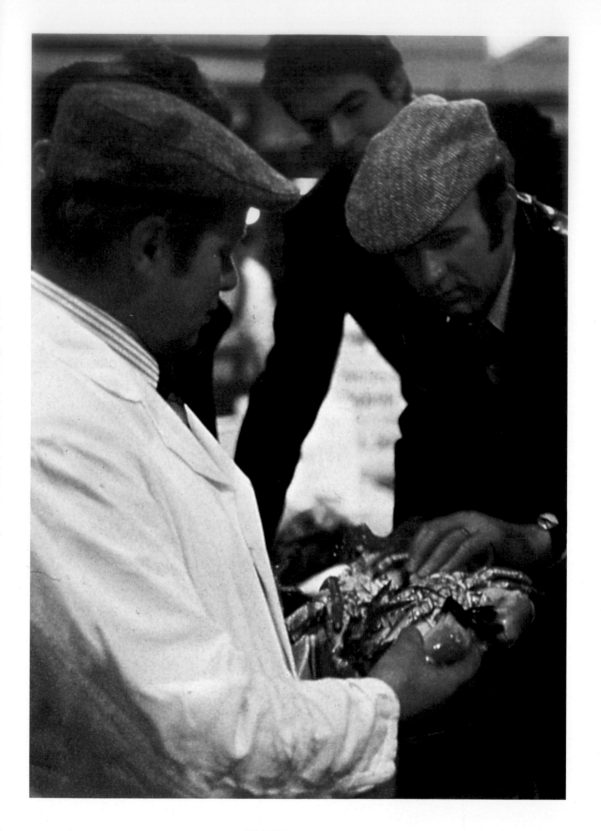

PLATE 4
Anton Mosimann inspecting freshly-cooked crab at London's Billingsgate fish market.

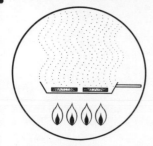

Shallow frying
Sauter

Often called pan frying, sautéd foods are fried quickly in a small amount of hot oil or butter in a shallow pan — a sauteuse. Mosly used for *à la minute* dishes. There are several possibilities in this method of preparation.

a) to fry in a sauteuse in hot oil as, for example, with small pieces of meat and poultry, fish goujons, vegetables, potatoes.

b) to fry both sides in hot oil or butter in a sautoir at 170°-230°C/340°-450°F, for example, entrecôte steaks, cutlets, chicken breasts, fish fillets.

In the preparation of meat, sharply falling temperatures must be avoided, otherwise the meat loses too much juice and becomes tough.

Note: The terms 'pan frying' and 'shallow frying' are often interchangeable, but a larger amount of fat is normally used for pan frying.

Heat transference agent	fat
Method of heat transference	conduction
Working temperature	160°-240°C/ 325°-475°F
Typical food	cutlets escalopes fish potatoes etc.
Typical cooking equipment	pan, sautoir, griddle tray grilling tray brat pan

Grilling
Griller

Grilling is a very wholesome method of preparation and can be carried out with either top or bottom open heat. Grilling over charcoal lends a particular taste to the food.

Only a small amount of oil should be used and the following points should be noted:

• To begin with, the temperature should be between 220°-260°C/430°-500°F, and towards the end it should be 150°-210°C/300°-410°F.

• The higher temperature will close the pores. Thin pieces of meat require more heat, thicker pieces a lower heat.

Grilling is suitable for small and medium sized fish, for pieces of meat such as entrecôte, châteaubriand, and also for vegetables, poultry.

Heat transference agent	air, fat
Method of heat transference	conduction radiation
Working temperature	220°-260°C/ 430°-500°F
Typical food	steaks meat fish poultry etc.
Typical cooking equipment	grill salamander grill roasting pan

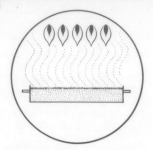

Gratinating
Gratiner

A process in which finished dishes are browned or glazed in the oven or under the grill at a high temperature with the heat coming from above (approx. 250°-300°C/480°-570°F). There must be a fatty substance (cream, cheese, egg or butter — or a mixture of these) covering the food. Suitable for soups, fish, meat, poultry, vegetables, potatoes, pasta.
Note: For uncooked food with a porous structure, browning comprises the whole cooking process. Browning may also be used for certain desserts, for example glazing of meringues.

Heat transference agent	air, fat
Method of heat transference	radiation
Working temperature	250°-300°C/ 480°-570°F
Typical food	fish
	meat
	poultry
	vegetables
	potatoes
	pasta (ravioli)
Typical cooking equipment	salamander
	hot air convection oven

Baking in the oven
Cuire au four

There are various methods:
a) on the grid at 140°-250°C/285°-480°F
b) on a baking tray at 170°-240°C/340°-460°F
Food may be baked in the oven without adding any liquid or fat; it can also be baked in moulds. Baking is particularly suitable for meat dishes such as ham in pastry, filet de boeuf Wellington, and for baked potatoes, pastry dishes, desserts, bread and pastry.

Heat transference agent	air
Method of heat transference	radiation
	conduction
	convection
Working temperature	140°-250°C/ 285°-480°F
Typical food	pastry baking
	confectionery
	meat
	poultry in pastry
Typical cooking equipment	oven
	hot air convection oven

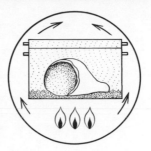

Roasting
Rôtir

Food should be roasted in the oven at 210°-250°C/
410°-480°F to start with and then finished at
150°-200°C/300°-390°F, basting continuously.
This method is very suitable for meat, poultry,
game, fish, potatoes.
On a spit the temperature should be 230°-280°C/
450°-535°F to start with and 160°-200°C/325°-
390°F to finish. The same principle is used as for
baking in the oven, except that a higher
temperature is necessary. Dark meat is particularly suitable for this basic method.

Heat transference agent	fat, air
Method of heat transference	conduction
Working temperature	180°-230°C/ 350°-450°F
Typical food	joints of meat poultry game potatoes etc.
Typical cooking equipment	roasting or baking oven brat pan grill (on spit) rôtissoir hot air convection oven with steam injection

Braising
Braiser

Braising is a gentle basic form of preparation in a
covered container in the oven at about 180°-
200°C (350°-390°F).
To braise red meat: Brown the meat quickly at a
fairly high temperature in a container, add the
mirepoix, remove the fat, add wine or marinade.
Allow to reduce considerably. Add brown veal
stock to approximately a quarter of the volume
and reduce in the oven until almost a glaze. Add
some stock as before. Cover and braise in the
oven. Baste and turn the meat occasionally.
Remove meat from the stock. Reduce the stock,
strain and pour back in the braisière over the
meat. Braise uncovered, with the heat coming
from above, basting constantly until tender.
Possibly monté the sauce with butter, and season
with salt and pepper.
Note: The more tender the meat the lower the
heat and the less liquid is required.

To braise fish and vegetables: Sweat vegetables
at a low heat, add a little stock or court-bouillon.
Add fish or vegetables and cover. Braise in the
oven at 140-160°C (275-325°F) basting occasionally. If necessary, keep adding liquid. Serve in
the liquid or use it for making a sauce.

Heat transference agent	fat, liquid
Method of heat transference	conduction condensation
Working temperature	180°-200°C/ 350°-390°F
Typical food	dark meat vegetables fish
Typical cooking equipment	casserole braisière brat pan, stove, oven convector

Glazing
Glacer

Glazing for white meat and poultry
Follow the basic preparation for braising, but use
a lower temperature and deglaze with white
wine. Add some brown stock and reduce to a
glaze. Add more stock to cover approximately
one sixth of the meat. Cover with a lid and baste
occasionally until nearly tender. Remove the lid
and glaze with the now syrup-thick stock, with
the heat coming from above, basting constantly.
Remove meat, add white wine and some stock.
Strain through a fine sieve, remove fat, and
season with salt and pepper.
Note: The brown stock forms a sticky crust which
prevents the meat juices from running out.

Glazing (for vegetables)
Add some sugar, butter, water or stock to the
vegetables, cover and glaze at a low temperature
of 150°-200°C (300°-392°F). When the liquid is
greatly reduced, remove the lid and stirring all
the time, glaze.
This method of preparing is particularly suitable
for vegetables containing sugar, such as carrots,
turnips, small onions.

Heat transference agent	fat, liquid
Method of heat transference	conduction condensation
Working temperature	160°-200°C 325°-390°F
Typical food	white meat poultry vegetables
Typical cooking equipment	stove casserole brat pan

Pot Roasting
Poêler

A process by which food is placed in a covered
pan in the oven with mirepoix and a generous
amount of butter at approximately 140°-210°C
(285°-410°).
Place the mirepoix in the pan with the meat or
poultry and the butter. Cover and poêlé slowly
in the oven in its own juice at a low temperature,
basting regularly.
Just before the end of the preparation time,
remove the lid and allow the meat to become
golden coloured. Remove the meat, add some
white wine and brown stock to the pan, and
reduce. Strain, skim and season to taste.
This method of preparation is particularly
suitable for poultry and tender pieces of
meat.

Heat transference agent	fat, air
Method of heat transference	conduction condensation
Working temperature	140°-210°C/ 285°-410°F
Typical food	poultry joints of meat
Typical cooking equipment	stove, roasting or baking oven, brat pan

Stewing
Etuver

To prepare meat, vegetables or fruit in a covered stewing pot, at a lower temperature than braising. Pour some melted butter into the container, place the food on top, cover, and stew on a low temperature 110°-140°C/230°-275°F. Reduce the liquid which has formed. Depending on the dish, the stock may be served as well. Particularly suitable for fish, small pieces of meat, vegetables, fruits.

Heat transference agent	partly liquid, partly fat and steam condensation
Method of heat transference	conduction
Working temperature	110°-140°C/ 230°-275°F
Typical food	vegetables veal fish mushrooms etc.
Typical cooking equipment	stove (casserole) brat pan hot air convection oven

Stocks, broths and pastes

In the past, stocks made from bones used to be cooked for eight to ten hours or sometimes even days. Today this is no longer necessary. There are various reasons for this: the fattening of animals is completely different, for example their food being based more on vitamins. As a result the animals are slaughtered earlier than they used to be. Nowadays all that remains after boiling the bones for too long is a glutinous liquid.

In order to produce a good sauce, it is absolutely essential to have a stock which has been prepared carefully and with love. In order to get the best from the bones, they should always be cut up small. For brown stocks the bones should always be boiled up with little liquid and then reduced almost to a glaze. This process should be repeated three or four times in order to give the stock a good strong colour.

Note: If a stock does become cloudy, the following should be noted:

Clarifying with the white of an egg

Mix a lightly beaten egg white with a few ice flakes or ice cubes and add to the warm stock. Bring to the boil, stirring constantly. The egg white will catch the particles and no small globules will form; the stock will become noticeably clearer. Strain through a cloth or fine sieve.

Clarifying with ice

Stir some ice flakes or ice cubes into the warm stock and bring to the boil, stirring constantly. The coldness will cause the solid air-saturated particles to come together and become heavy. Strain through a cloth or fine sieve.

Use of Recipes
Numbers of recipes are given at the foot of each page. They refer to each complete or continued recipe on that page.

Fond blanc de volaille
White poultry stock

Ingredients (for 1 litre of poultry stock)

1		boiling fowl (blanched)
2 litres	(3½ pints)	water
50g	(2oz)	white bouquet garni (onion, white of leek, celeriac and herbs)
		salt, freshly ground pepper

Method
- Put the boiling fowl in a saucepan, fill up with cold water, bring to the boil and skim.
- Add the bouquet garni and seasoning.
- Leave to simmer carefully for 2 hours, occasionally skimming and removing the fat.
- Strain the stock through a fine cloth or sieve and season to taste.

Note The boiling fowl can afterwards be used for various cold dishes.

Fond blanc de veau
White veal stock

Ingredients (for 1 litre of veal stock)

1kg	(2lb)	finely chopped veal bone, cut in small pieces
2 litres	(3½ pints)	water
50g	(2oz)	white bouquet garni (see recipe 1)
		salt, freshly ground pepper

▶

Method

- Place the blanched bones in cold water, bring to the boil and skim.
- Add the bouquet garni and seasoning.
- Leave to simmer for 2 hours, occasionally skimming and removing the fat.
- Strain the stock through a cloth or fine sieve and season to taste.

Note Calves' feet and/or veal trimmings may be used instead of veal bone.

Fond brun de volaille
Brown poultry stock

Ingredients (for 1 litre of poultry stock)

1kg	(2lb)	poultry bones and trimmings, cut in small pieces
2cl	(¾fl oz)	oil
50g	(2oz)	mirepoix (see page 296)
50g	(2oz)	diced tomatoes
30cl	(½ pint)	white wine
2 litres	(3½ pints)	water
		salt, freshly ground pepper

Method

- Roast the bones and trimmings with the oil in a stewpan in the oven until brown.
- Remove the oil with a spoon or strain off, add the mirepoix and tomatoes and continue to roast carefully for a further 4 to 5 minutes.
- First, add the white wine and then 50cl (18fl oz) of water, bring to the boil and reduce.
- Add the same amount of water again and reduce to a glaze. ▶

- Remove from the oven and transfer to a saucepan.
- Add the remaining water and simmer carefully for 2 hours, occasionally skimming and removing the fat.
- Strain through a cloth or fine sieve and season to taste.

Note By means of repeated reduction a strong, deeply coloured stock is obtained (See also recipe 4).

Fond brun de veau
Brown veal stock

Ingredients (for 1 litre of veal stock)

1kg	(2lb)	veal bones and trimmings, cut in small pieces
2cl	(¾floz)	oil
50g	(2oz)	mirepoix (see page 296)
500g	(18oz)	diced tomatoes
1.5 litres	(2½ pints)	clear brown stock (see recipe 11)
1 litre	(1¾ pints)	water
		salt, freshly ground pepper

Method
- Roast the veal bones and trimmings with the oil in a roasting pan in the oven until brown.
- Remove the oil with a spoon or strain off, add the mirepoix and tomatoes and roast for another 4 to 5 minutes.
- Add half the clear brown stock and bring to the boil.
- Add the remaining stock and reduce to a glaze.
- Remove from the oven and transfer to a saucepan.
- Add the water and simmer for 2 hours, occasionally skimming and removing the fat.
- Strain through a cloth or fine sieve and season to taste.

Fond d'agneau
Lamb stock

Ingredients (for 1 litre of lamb stock)

1kg	(2lb)	lamb bones, chopped finely
2 litres	(3½ pints)	water
50g	(2oz)	white bouquet garni (see recipe 1)
		some parsley stalks
		salt, freshly ground pepper

Method

- Put the blanched bones into cold water, boil up and skim.
- Add the bouquet garni, parsley stalks and seasoning.
- Allow to simmer for 1 hour, occasionally removing the fat and skimming.
- Strain the stock through a muslin and season.

Note Lambs' feet or lamb trimmings can also be used with the lamb bones.

Fond de poisson
Fish stock

Ingredients (for 1 litre of fish stock)

1kg	(2lb)	broken up fish bones and trimmings
50g	(2oz)	white mirepoix (onions, white of leek, celeriac, fennel leaves, dill)
30g	(1¼oz)	mushroom trimmings
20g	(¾oz)	butter
20cl	(6fl oz)	white wine
1.2 litres	(2 pints)	water
		salt, freshly ground pepper

▶

Method
- Thoroughly wash the fish bones and trimmings.
- Sweat the mirepoix and the mushroom trimmings in the butter.
- Add the fish bones and trimmings, white wine and water.
- Simmer for 20 minutes, occasionally skimming and removing the fat.
- Strain through a cloth or fine sieve and season with salt and pepper.

Note In order to produce a good fish stock, only the bones of fresh white fish (sole, turbot) should be used.

Court-bouillon
Stock for poaching fish

Ingredients (for 2 litres of water)

50cl	(18fl oz)	dry white wine
200g	(7oz)	carrots, finely cut
100g	(4oz)	white leek, finely cut
100g	(4oz)	onions, finely cut
50g	(2oz)	celery, finely cut
1		clove of garlic, unpeeled
5		stalks of parsley
1		small sprig of thyme
½		bay leaf
5		crushed white peppercorns
3		coriander seeds
		salt

Method
- Bring the water and white wine to the boil.
- Add all the ingredients and allow to simmer for 10 minutes.

Fond de moules
Mussel stock

Ingredients (for 1 litre of mussel stock)

1.5kg	(3lb)	mussels, scraped and washed
8cl	(3fl oz)	water
8cl	(3fl oz)	dry white wine
10g	(½oz)	finely chopped shallot
10g	(½oz)	diced celery
		a few parsley stalks
		a little thyme
		freshly ground pepper

Method

- Prepare the mussels.
- Bring the water, wine, shallot, celery cubes, parsley and thyme to the boil in a suitable pan.
- Add the mussels, season with pepper.
- Cover and allow to boil for 3 to 4 minutes (until the mussels open, not allowing them to become tough).
- Remove the mussels from the stock with a sieve or skimming ladle and use elsewhere when needed.
- Allow the stock to stand for 3 to 4 minutes, and then strain through a fine muslin.

Note It is important to strain the stock carefully so that no sand remains in it.

Glace de viande
Meat glaze

Reduce 10 litres (16 pints) of brown veal stock or clear brown stock (recipe 11) to 1 litre (1¾ pints) in a suitable saucepan on low heat. During reduction keep transferring the liquid into smaller saucepans. It is important that the edge of the saucepan is kept clean by means of a spatula.

Note Similar glazes can be made from fish, poultry and game.

Fond de gibier
Game stock

Ingredients (for 1 litre of game stock)

1kg	(2lb)	finely chopped game bones and trimmings
2cl	(¾fl oz)	oil
50g	(2oz)	mirepoix (see page 296)
4-5		juniper berries
30cl	(½ pint)	white wine
1 litre	(1¾ pints)	brown veal stock (see recipe 4)
1.5 litres	(2½ pints)	water
		salt, freshly ground pepper

Method
- Roast the bones and trimmings with the oil in a stew pan until brown.
- Remove the oil with a spoon or strain off, add the mirepoix and juniper berries and continue to roast for a further 4 to 5 minutes. ▶

- Remove from the oven and transfer to a saucepan.
- Add the white wine and reduce.
- Add the brown veal stock and reduce to a glaze.
- Add the water and simmer slowly for 1½ hours, occasionally skimming and removing the fat.
- Strain through a cloth or fine sieve and season to taste.

Note By means of repeated reduction a strong, deeply coloured stock is obtained.

Bouillon de viande
Meat broth

Ingredients (for 1 litre of broth)
1kg	(2lb)	chopped beef bones
200g	(7oz)	lean beef trimmings
50g	(2oz)	bouquet garni
½		browned onion
2 litres	(3½ pints)	water
		salt, freshly ground pepper

Method
- Place the soaked, and if necessary blanched, bones and meat in a saucepan of cold water, bring to the boil and skim.
- Add the remaining ingredients.
- Simmer for 2 hours, occasionally skimming and removing the fat.
- Strain the broth through a cloth or fine sieve and season to taste.

Note In order to give the broth a good colour, the onions are browned in their skin.

Fond de canard sauvage
Wild duck stock

Ingredients (for 1 litre of duck stock)

1kg	(2lb)	carcase of wild duck
30g	(1¼oz)	finely chopped bacon
50g	(2oz)	chopped shallots
50g	(2oz)	diced carrot
20g	(¾oz)	diced celery
50g	(2oz)	mushroom trimmings
1		bay leaf
1		sprig of thyme
10		juniper berries
1		clove
20g	(¾oz)	diced tomato
10g	(½oz)	parsley trimmings
1cl	(½fl oz)	vinegar
20cl	(6fl oz)	red wine
1 litre	(1¾ pints)	game stock (see recipe 10)
		salt, freshly ground pepper

Method

- Chop up the duck carcase.
- Gently sauté the finely chopped bacon in a suitable pan.
- Add the chopped duck carcase and fry until brown.
- Pour off the cooking fat and add the shallot, carrot, celery and mushroom trimmings.
- Continue to sauté without letting it colour.
- Add the bay leaf, thyme, juniper berries, clove, tomato and parsley.
- Roast in a moderately warm oven for 10 to 15 minutes.
- Add the vinegar and red wine and reduce completely.
- Add the game stock, season with salt and allow to simmer for 1 hour, occasionally skimming the stock.
- Finally strain through a fine sieve, allow to reduce a little and season with salt and pepper.

Fond de légumes
Vegetable stock

Ingredients (for 1 litre of vegetable stock)

30g	(1¼oz)	butter	
40g	(1½oz)	onions	
40g	(1½oz)	leeks	
20g	(¾oz)	celery	} cut up and
30g	(1¼oz)	cabbage	finely chopped
20g	(¾oz)	fennel	
30g	(1¼oz)	tomatoes	
1.5 litres	(2½ pints)	water	
½		bay leaf	
½		clove	
		salt, freshly ground pepper	

Method
- Melt the butter and sweat the onions and leeks in it.
- Add the remaining vegetables and sweat for a further 10 minutes.
- Add the water with the bay leaf and clove and simmer for 20 minutes.
- Strain through a cloth or fine sieve and season to taste.

Note This is usually used for soups and vegetarian dishes.

Mousseline de brochet
Mousseline of pike

Ingredients (for 4 people)

250g	(9oz)	pike flesh, without skin and bones
		salt, freshly ground pepper
		a little cayenne and nutmeg
30cl	(½ pint)	double cream

Method
- Mince the pike flesh finely and place in a bowl on ice.
- Season with salt, pepper, nutmeg and cayenne.
- Work in the double cream, using a wooden spoon.
- Press the mixture through a hair sieve and keep cool.
- Season again and store in a cool place.

Note It is very important that the double cream is worked in slowly and thoroughly so that the cream and pike flesh bind together. This mousseline may be used for quenelles and also as stuffing for such dishes as tronçon de turbot (recipe 87).

Mousseline de volaille
Mousseline of chicken

Ingredients (for 4 people)

150g	(5oz)	white poultry meat, well timmed
35cl	(12fl oz)	double cream
		salt, freshly ground pepper

Method
- Finely mince the well trimmed meat (with sinews removed) and then press through a fine sieve. ▶

- Place in a bowl on ice.
- Vigorously mix in the cream, a little at a time so that a light, airy farce is produced.
- Season with salt and pepper.

Farce à gratin
Forcemeat for game

Ingredients (for 250g (9oz) farce)

200g	(7oz)	meat from feathered game
2cl	(¾fl oz)	peanut oil
100g	(4oz)	liver from feathered game
10g	(½oz)	butter
5g	(¼oz)	shallot, finely chopped
50g	(2oz)	mushrooms, chopped finely
2cl	(¾fl oz)	double cream
1cl	(½fl oz)	Cognac
1cl	(½fl oz)	Madeira
		salt, freshly ground pepper

Method
- Sauté the seasoned meat in oil and leave to cool.
- Sauté the seasoned liver in butter and also leave to cool.
- When cool, mince the meat and liver with the sautéd shallots and mushrooms.
- Then press through a hair sieve. Place in a bowl on ice.
- Gradually mix in the cream.
- Finish with Cognac and Madeira wine.
- Season with salt and pepper.

Note This farce is mainly used with game and served on croûtons (slices of toasted French bread). It is a good idea to brown the croûtons and farce under the grill just before serving.

Pâte à brioche
Brioche paste

Ingredients (for 10 people)

10g	(½oz)	yeast
2.5cl	(1fl oz)	milk
250g	(9oz)	flour, sieved
		pinch of salt
150g	(5oz)	butter
10g	(½oz)	sugar
150g	(5oz)	eggs (3)

Method

- Dissolve the yeast in lukewarm milk.
- Make the leaven with 100g (4oz) of flour, salt and dissolved yeast.
- Allow to ferment for 1 to 1½ hours in a warm place.
- Meanwhile mix the butter with the sugar until soft and add the eggs.
- Make the paste with the remaining flour, salt and butter and egg mixture.
- Knead it until air bubbles are formed.
- Knead in the leaven, cover and allow to ferment for 15 to 20 minutes in a warm place.
- After fermenting beat the paste.
- Place the mixture in brioche moulds until one third full.
- Before baking allow to ferment again in a warm place for 20 minutes.
- Bake until golden brown for 25 minutes in a hot oven at 220°-230° C (425°-450°F).

Note This paste should double in volume after fermentation.

Pâte brisée
Shortcrust paste

Ingredients

220g	(8oz)	flour, sieved
150g	(5oz)	butter
1		egg
5cl	(2fl oz)	milk
15g	(½oz)	salt

Method

- With the fingers rub together the butter, sieved flour and salt.
- Mix in the egg and cold milk.
- Knead all together.
- Rest the paste for an hour before rolling out.

Pâte feuilletée
Puff paste

Ingredients

450g	(1lb)	flour, sieved
20cl	(6fl oz)	water
15g	(½oz)	salt
500g	(18oz)	butter

Method (see also illustrations opposite)

- Make a firm and well kneaded paste out of the sieved flour, water and salt.
- Allow to rest for 30 minutes.
- Roll out the paste to a square about 2cm (¾in) thick.
- Press the butter until fairly flat, place in the middle of the paste so that the edges of the paste are lying opposite the sides of the butter. ▶

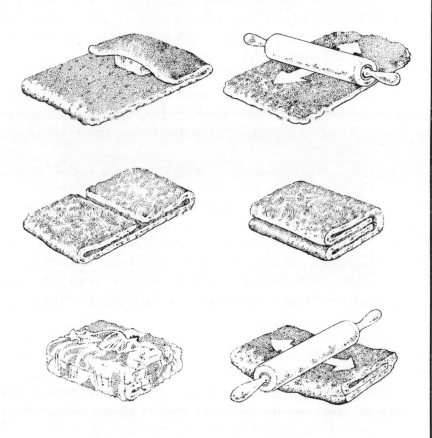

Pâte feuilletée

Top to bottom, left to right:
Fold the paste to enclose the butter; roll into a long rectangle; fold the ends to the centre; fold in half; rolling and folding into 3 thicknesses completes one single turn; finally, the paste should rest for at least 2 hours before rolling.

- Fold the edges of the paste over the butter so that it is completely enclosed in it.
- Roll the paste and butter into a long rectangle 2cm (¾in) thick.
- Fold the two ends of the paste evenly towards the centre so that they meet in the middle of the paste.
- Then fold over both halves of the paste so that the middle now becomes one of the sides. This is one double turn.
- Roll the paste and butter into a rectangle, lay one third of the paste over the middle third and cover this part with the other third so that the paste, which is 2-3cm (¾-1¼in) thick, is in 3 layers (this is called a single turn).
- Puff paste requires 4 double turns or 6 single turns.
- Between each turn the paste should rest for 20 minutes in a cool place. For feuilleté one more double or single turn should be made. The paste should rest for at least 2 hours before use so that it can be rolled out regularly. The paste must be firm and a sharp knife should be used to make a clean cut. This can, of course, also be done with a pastry cutter.

Note As can be seen from the above recipe, puff paste should be turned so as always to produce a layer of butter between two layers of paste. The layers should on no account be damaged through inexpert handling. Since butter contains 60 per cent water, steam is therefore produced during baking. Between every second layer of paste, therefore, a steam 'pillow' is formed which causes the paste to rise. Therefore puff paste will rise well as long as the paste is laid in perfect layers.

Pâte feuilletée rapide
Lightning puff pastry

This is the shortest time required for the making of puff pastry, using the useful lightning method. The ingredients remain the same as for the basic recipe.

Method
500g (18oz) of butter should be kept cold and then cut into nut-sized cubes. These butter cubes should then be mixed in with the flour; 20cl (6fl oz) water and salt is added and then it is kneaded into a paste, with the butter remaining in cubes in the paste. After a pause of at least five minutes, the paste may be given four double turns.

Note It is advisable for all the pieces of puff paste which are going to be used to rest in the freezer. It is even a good idea, for example, to place a feuilleté on a piece of greaseproof paper on a baking tray while still frozen and then to bake in the oven. The paste loses some liquid whereby steam is produced and this makes it much lighter when baked.

Pâte sucrée
Sugar paste

Ingredients

250g	(9oz)	flour, sieved
2.5g		baking powder
100g	(4oz)	butter
100g	(4oz)	sugar
2		egg yolks
		a little water
		zest of ¼ lemon

►

Method

- Make a well in the middle of the flour and baking powder.
- Vigorously work in the butter, sugar, egg yolks, water and lemon zest towards the middle of the well.
- Continue to knead the mixture and work into a smooth paste.

Note This paste should be completed as quickly as possible. It is used for many recipes requiring sweet pastry and particularly for Florentines (see recipe 202).

Pâte à ravioli
Ravioli paste

Ingredients (for 4 people)

100g	(4oz)	flour, sieved
30g	(1¼oz)	semolina
½		egg
1cl	(½fl oz)	oil
		pinch of salt
5cl	(2fl oz)	water

Method

- Make a well in the mixed flour and semolina.
- Place the egg, oil, salt and water in the well.
- Gradually mix the flour in towards the middle.
- Knead the mixture to a smooth firm paste.

Note This paste should rest for 1-2 hours before use.

Nouilles aux épinards
Homemade egg noodles with spinach

Ingredients (for 4 people)

200g	(7oz)	flour, sieved
25g	(1oz)	semolina
1cl	(½fl oz)	oil
1		egg
3.5g		salt
50g	(2oz)	purée of spinach
		possibly a little water

Method

- Make a well in the mixed flour and semolina.
- Place the other ingredients in the well.
- Gradually work the flour and semolina in towards the middle and knead into a very firm, smooth dough.
- Wrap in a damp cloth and allow to rest in a cool place for at least 2-3 hours.
- Divide the dough into five pieces and roll out each piece as thinly as possible.
- Lay the pieces of dough on top of each other and cut into strips approximately 6-7mm (¼in) wide.
- These noodles may be cooked while fresh or kept to dry out.

Note It is important that the noodles are always cooked *al dente*. After draining, rinse with cold water, sauté in butter, season and serve immediately. If the noodles are not used immediately, they may be kept on a board in an airy place to dry out.

Chapter 2

Sauces

Sauces

A good chef can be recognised by his sauces. In the orchestra of a great kitchen the *saucier* is a soloist, for good sauces are the perfect accompaniment to individual dishes. Indeed the variety of sauces is the basic wealth of a good kitchen. A carefully prepared stock forms the basis for a fine sauce.

Nowadays sauces are made much lighter without flour. By reducing the stock a strong sauce is obtained, and this is finished with either cream or butter. Possibly the sauce may be thickened with a binding agent or beaten up in a mixer (so that it becomes light). Most sauces are prepared *à la minute*, at the last moment, and only in the quantity needed.

Sauce de homard
Lobster sauce

Ingredients (for 4 people)

1		lobster (250-300g (9-10oz))
5cl	(2fl oz)	olive oil
50g	(2oz)	mirepoix (see page 296)
50g	(2oz)	diced tomatoes
5cl	(2fl oz)	Cognac
10cl	(4fl oz)	white wine
50cl	(18fl oz)	fish stock (see recipe 6)
		a little fresh dill and tarragon
		a little meat glaze (see recipe 9)
50g	(2oz)	butter
		salt, freshly ground pepper

Method

- Place the lobster in boiling water for one minute to kill it.
- Cut the body in half and chop into pieces, remove stomach and save the coral.
- Heat the olive oil in a sautoir, add the lobster pieces and, using a wooden spatula, sauté on all sides (until the shell is completely red).
- Add the mirepoix and tomatoes and sweat well.
- Flame with the brandy and then add the white wine.
- Add the fish stock and chopped herbs and bring to the boil.
- Take the lobster pieces and remove the meat from the shell.
- Cut up the lobster shell as finely as possible and return to the stock.
- Simmer for approximately 30 minutes on a low heat.
- Add the meat glaze and reduce the stock to one third its original volume.

►

- Add the lobster coral, mixed with the butter, to bind it.
- Strain the sauce and season to taste.

Note The lobster meat may be used for various other dishes, for instance, in a cold buffet.

Sauce aux écrevisses
Crayfish sauce

Ingredients (for 1 litre of crayfish sauce)

20		freshwater crayfish
60g	(2½oz)	butter
15g	(½oz)	shallots, finely chopped
10cl	(4fl oz)	dry white wine
50g	(2oz)	tomatoes, diced
		a little tarragon and thyme
1cl	(½fl oz)	meat glaze (see recipe 9)
50cl	(18fl oz)	fish stock (see recipe 6)
20cl	(6fl oz)	single cream
		salt, cayenne and freshly ground pepper

Method
- Blanch the cleaned crayfish in boiling water for 15 seconds.
- Remove immediately.
- Put the butter in a saucepan, add the shallots and sweat.
- Add the crayfish and sauté.
- Add the white wine.
- Add the diced tomatoes, tarragon and thyme and bring to the boil.
- Remove the crayfish after 2 minutes, break open and remove the intestine.

▶

- Finely crush the crayfish bodies and add to the stock.
- Add the meat glaze and fish stock and allow to simmer for 30 minutes.
- Finally, pass through a fine muslin, add the cream and boil up again.
- Season the sauce with salt, pepper and cayenne.

Sauce Western
Western sauce

Ingredients (for 4 people)

5g	(¼oz)	shallots, finely chopped
20g	(¾oz)	butter
100g	(4oz)	raw mushrooms, sliced
80g	(3¼oz)	small raw morels, cleaned thoroughly
50g	(2oz)	small raw chanterelles, cleaned thoroughly
40g	(1½oz)	walnuts, blanched, peeled and coarsely chopped
3cl	(1fl oz)	whisky
5cl	(2fl oz)	white wine
40cl	(¾ pint)	brown veal stock (see recipe 4) a little tarragon, finely chopped
50g	(2oz)	butter, to finish salt, freshly ground pepper

Method
- Sweat the shallots in butter.
- Add the mushrooms, morels, chanterelles and walnuts and continue to sweat.
- Add the whisky and white wine and reduce a little.
- Add the brown veal stock and reduce a little.
- Add the chopped tarragon and monté with butter.
- Season with salt and freshly ground pepper.

Recipes 24 & 25

Sauce hollandaise
Hollandaise sauce

Ingredients (for 4 people)

2cl	(¾fl oz)	vinegar
15g	(½oz)	shallots, finely chopped
2-3		crushed peppercorns
2cl	(¾fl oz)	water
3		egg yolks
200g	(7oz)	melted and clarified butter (see page 294)
		a little salt, freshly ground pepper
		a little lemon juice

Method

- In a small saucepan, almost completely reduce the vinegar, shallots and crushed peppercorns.
- Add the cold water and egg yolks and, stirring constantly over simmering water, work into a thick binding cream.
- Place the bowl in a moderately warm place and very gradually work in the melted butter (55°C (131°F)), stirring all the time.
- Season the sauce with salt, pepper and lemon juice.
- Finally, strain through a muslin sieve and use as required.

Note For vegetables such as asparagus and artichokes the hollandaise sauce should be prepared with tarragon vinegar and white wine.

Sauce aux truffes
Truffle sauce

Ingredients (for 4 people)

20cl	(6fl oz)	Madeira
10cl	(4fl oz)	Port
5cl	(2fl oz)	truffle stock (juice from bottled truffles)
2g		finely chopped shallot
50cl	(18fl oz)	brown veal stock (see recipe 4)
40g	(1½oz)	butter to finish
		salt, freshly ground pepper
2g		truffles, finely chopped

Method

- Reduce the Madeira, Port, truffle stock and shallot until almost a glaze.
- Add the brown veal stock and reduce until the required consistency is achieved.
- Monté with butter, add the finely chopped truffles and season with salt and pepper.

Sauce marchand de vin
Red wine sauce with shallots

Ingredients (for 4 people)

100g	(4oz)	finely chopped shallots
10g	(½oz)	butter
2		garlic cloves, unpeeled
1		small sprig of thyme
¼		bay leaf
5g	(¼oz)	crushed peppercorns
40cl	(¾ pint)	red wine (Burgundy)
30cl	(½ pint)	brown veal stock (see recipe 4)

▶

50g	(2oz)	meat extract (see recipe 9)
40g	(1½oz)	butter, to finish
		salt, freshly ground pepper

Method
- Sweat the finely chopped shallots in the butter.
- Add the garlic, thyme, bay leaf and peppercorns.
- Add the red wine and reduce almost completely.
- Add the brown veal stock.
- Add the meat extract and reduce to half its original volume.
- Strain through a fine sieve and carefully monté with the soft butter.
- Season with salt and pepper.

Sauce de gibier
Game sauce

Ingredients (for 4 people)

10cl	(4fl oz)	Madeira
20cl	(6fl oz)	ruby Port
10cl	(4fl oz)	Cognac
		thyme, bay leaf
		a little orange peel
10		juniper berries
40cl	(¾ pint)	game stock (see recipe 10)
40g	(1½oz)	butter
80g	(3¼oz)	chicken liver parfait (see recipe 51)
10cl	(4fl oz)	veal blood
2cl	(¾fl oz)	double cream
		salt, freshly ground pepper

Method
- Heat the Madeira, Port and 5cl (2fl oz) Cognac with the thyme, bay leaf, orange peel and juniper berries, flambé and almost completely reduce.

▶

- Add the game stock and allow to reduce a little more.
- With a fork, mix together the soft butter, chicken liver parfait and veal blood.
- Gradually and carefully add this mixture to the sauce.
- Add the remaining Cognac and cream.
- Strain through a fine sieve and season with salt and pepper.

Note This sauce should not be 'cooked' again after it has been bound with the blood.

Sauce madère
Madeira sauce

Ingredients (for 4 people)

10g	(½oz)	finely chopped shallot
10g	(½oz)	butter
1		small sprig of thyme
¼		bay leaf
8cl	(3fl oz)	Madeira
30cl	(½ pint)	brown veal stock (see recipe 4)
20g	(¾oz)	meat extract (see recipe 9)
40g	(1½oz)	butter, to finish
		salt, freshly ground pepper

Method
- Sweat the finely chopped shallot in butter, without letting it colour.
- Add the thyme and bay leaf.
- Add the Madeira and allow to reduce almost completely.
- Add the brown veal stock and the meat extract and reduce again.
- Strain through a fine sieve and gradually add the soft butter.
- Season with salt and pepper.

Sauce Foyot
Foyot sauce

Ingredients (for 4 people)

10cl	(4fl oz)	tarragon vinegar
20g	(¾oz)	chopped shallots
2g		crushed peppercorns
10cl	(4fl oz)	white wine
3		egg yolks
200g	(7oz)	melted and clarified butter
		a little salt and freshly ground pepper
		a few chopped tarragon leaves
2cl	(¾fl oz)	meat glaze to garnish (see recipe 9)

Method
- Make a reduction out of the vinegar, shallots and peppercorns.
- Add the white wine and egg yolks, put in a bain-marie on a gentle heat and, stirring constantly, monté to a thick binding cream.
- Place the pan on a moderate heat and slowly mix in the melted butter, stirring constantly.
- Season the sauce with salt and pepper.
- Finally strain through a muslin and add the finely chopped tarragon.
- Arrange in a suitable dish and garnish attractively with the meat glaze.

Note The dish or bowl used for serving the sauce Foyot should not be too hot, otherwise the sauce will curdle.

Sauce au curry
Curry sauce

Ingredients (for 4 people)

30g	(1¼oz)	finely chopped onion
20g	(¾oz)	butter
30g	(1¼oz)	apple, peeled and cut into small pieces
30g	(1¼oz)	banana, peeled and cut in small pieces
10g	(½oz)	curry powder
2g		curry paste
10cl	(4fl oz)	white wine
40cl	(¾ pint)	chicken stock (see recipe 3)
20g	(¾oz)	mango chutney
		salt and freshly ground black pepper
1g		cornflower
4cl	(1½fl oz)	double cream
40g	(1½oz)	peanut butter to finish

Method

- Sweat the finely chopped onion in butter carefully, without giving it any colour.
- Prepare the apple and banana and sweat until all liquid is evaporated.
- Add the curry powder and curry paste.
- Add the white wine and reduce by half.
- Add the chicken stock and mango chutney.
- Season with salt and pepper.
- Allow to simmer for about 20-25 minutes.
- Strain through a small sieve and reduce.
- Mix well in a blender and reduce again to the required consistency.
- Mix the cornflower and cream together and add the sauce.
- Monté with the soft peanut butter.
- Season again with salt and pepper.

Beurre de basilic
Basil butter

Ingredients (for 4 people)

100g	(4oz)	butter
10g	(½oz)	fresh basil, with stalks removed
		salt, freshly ground pepper
		a little lemon juice

Method

- Mix the butter with the finely chopped basil and season with salt and pepper.
- Finish with lemon juice.

Note This butter may be stored in the refrigerator and used to finish various sauces.

Beurre de pistache
Pistachio butter

Ingredients (for 4 people)

80g	(3oz)	butter
30g	(1¼oz)	pistachio nuts, blanched and peeled
2cl	(¾fl oz)	Kirsch
3cl	(1fl oz)	double cream
		a little bitter almond flavouring
		salt, freshly ground pepper

Method

- Beat the butter until creamy.
- Make the pistachio nuts and kirsch into a purée.
- Mix this and the cream into the butter, season with bitter almond flavouring, salt and pepper.

Note The butter should always be served while creamy — it should not become too hard.

Beurre d'écrevisses
Crayfish butter

Ingredients (for 4 people)

100g	(4oz)	crayfish shells, crushed
150g	(5oz)	butter
		salt, freshly ground pepper
		a little Cognac

Method
- Beat the crayfish shells and butter into a pulp.
- Put the pulp into a saucepan and stir constantly over a gentle heat until the butter is clarified.
- Fill up with water, strain and put in a cool place.
- In a few hours the butter will have separated from the water and can be removed easily.
- Boil up the butter again and season with salt and pepper.
- Add the Cognac and strain through fine muslin.

Note Lobster butter is made in the same way. Instead of crayfish shells, lobster shells that are as red as possible should be used.

‘ The art of cooking depends for its development on the psychological state of society and has to follow the impulses received from it. When there are no problems in the way of developing a pleasant life, when wealth is assured for the future, in a word, when one doesn't have to think about money, the art of cooking has the best chance of developing because it is the most important factor in one of the most agreeable pleasures given to mankind — eating. ’

Recipe 35

Tomates concassées
Chopped tomatoes

Ingredients (for 4 people)

1kg	(2lb)	tomatoes (well ripened)
20g	(¾oz)	finely chopped shallot
2		whole cloves of garlic, unpeeled
1cl	(½fl oz)	olive oil
		some oregano and thyme
		salt, freshly ground pepper

Method

- Remove the stalks from the tomatoes and then blanch in hot water for approximately 12 seconds.
- Cut the peeled tomatoes in half, remove the pips and chop in small pieces.
- Sweat the finely chopped shallot and garlic well in the olive oil, without letting it colour.
- Add the tomatoes and herbs and season with salt and pepper.
- Cover and steam carefully for 25 minutes until soft and all the liquid evaporated.
- Remove the garlic cloves and, if necessary, season again with salt and pepper.

Note To obtain a pulp, pass the tomates concassées through a sieve.

Chapter 3

Hors d'oeuvre

Hors d'oeuvre

Small hors d'oeuvre represent the prelude to a meal of several courses. They are, so to speak, served at the edge of the actual menu, i.e. as small incidental dishes, as a foretaste of what is to come. Served before the meal, they should make a clear contrast to it. On no account should they really appease the appetite, so they must be varied, light and interesting and colourfully arranged. A chef's goal when he is preparing a beautiful dish should always and only be attained by the addition of extras which are edible and harmoniously arranged. Nothing should appear on the plate which is not edible and tastiness and simplicity should be the keynotes of the dish and the personality of the chef should be brought out in its style.

Méli-mélo de homard aux pointes d'asperges
Lobster salad with asparagus

Ingredients (for 4 people)

1.5 litres	(2½ pints)	stock (see below)
2		small lobsters weighing 250g (9oz) each
200g	(7oz)	haricots verts
50g	(2oz)	fresh yellow cèpes
50g	(2oz)	fresh chanterelles
1cl	(½fl oz)	olive oil
8		green asparagus tips
		salt, freshly ground pepper
1		lettuce, washed and dried
2		red chicory heads
4		slices of truffle
16		basil leaves

Stock

1 litre	(1¾ pints)	water
30cl	(½ pint)	dry white wine
12		crushed peppercorns
		a little thyme
¼		bay leaf
50g	(2oz)	onions, cut up into small pieces
40g	(1½oz)	carrots, cut up into small pieces
		salt, freshly ground pepper

Sauce vinaigrette

10cl	(4fl oz)	hazelnut oil
2cl	(¾fl oz)	Sherry vinegar
5g	(¼oz)	finely chopped shallot
		salt, freshly ground pepper

▶

Recipe 37

Method (See Plate 5)

- To prepare the stock, bring the water and white wine to the boil.
- Add the peppercorns, thyme, bay leaf, onions and carrots and simmer for 10 minutes. Season to taste.
- Put the lobsters into the stock and simmer for 5 minutes.
- Remove and keep lukewarm.
- Wash the beans thoroughly, cook until crisp and then plunge immediately into cold water.
- Wash the cèpes and chanterelles thoroughly and sauté in the olive oil. Keep lukewarm and put to one side.
- Prepare the asparagus tips and cook until crisp. Season to taste.
- Arrange the lettuce and the red chicory attractively on a plate.
- Also arrange the french beans, cèpes, chanterelles and asparagus tips.
- Remove the lobster flesh from the shell, cut into small pieces and arrange on the lettuce.
- To make the vinaigrette, mix together all the ingredients. Sprinkle over the salad and garnish with slices of truffle.
- Finally, sprinkle the basil leaves over the salad.

Note It is important that the lobster, cèpes, chanterelles, haricots verts and asparagus tips are still lukewarm when served.

‘ Food as it affects a man's health, temper and happiness still plays its great part in the world. If we are given to prayer it might be better that we pray for the skill and good judgement of the chef of a head of state than for the good councillors of many rulers of the earth. ’

Salade d'artichauts aux cailles
Artichoke salad with quails

Ingredients (for 4 people)

2		quails
20g	(¾oz)	butter
		salt, freshly ground pepper
6		juniper berries
2cl	(¾fl oz)	poultry stock (see recipe 1)
2		artichoke hearts (see page 256)
60g	(2½oz)	raw goose liver, cut into slices
60g	(2½oz)	small, raw yellow boletus (cèpes) cut into slices
16		grapes, peeled and stoned
4		walnuts, peeled and quartered
		vinaigrette sauce (see recipe 39)
		a few chervil leaves

Method

- Pluck, draw, singe and bind the quails.
- Put the butter into a suitable pan and sauté the seasoned quails, with the juniper berries, until pink.
- Remove the breasts, cook the legs slowly.
- Cut the breasts and legs into slices.
- Discard the fat and add the poultry stock (the cooking juices will be added to the sauce).
- Cut the artichoke hearts into eight pieces.
- Season the slices of goose liver and sauté until pink in a hot pan without fat.
- Mix the quail meat, goose liver, boletus, grapes and walnuts with the vinaigrette.
- Season to taste and arrange attractively.
- Garnish with the chervil leaves.

Salade de foie gras moderne
French goose liver salad

Ingredients (for 4 people)

160g	(5½oz)	raw goose liver
150g	(5oz)	small chanterelles
100g	(4oz)	small mushrooms
2cl	(¾fl oz)	olive oil
20g	(¾oz)	watercress
12		crisp lettuce leaves
80g	(3¼oz)	fine green beans, well blanched
		salt, freshly ground pepper

Method

- With a sharp knife, peel the goose livers and remove the nerves (see recipe 49).
- Cut into cubes measuring approximately 1.5cm (½in) season and fry quickly in a hot pan (without oil). Leave to drain.
- Season the raw chanterelles and mushrooms and sweat for a few minutes in the olive oil.
- While still warm mix the goose livers, chanterelles, mushrooms and watercress with vinaigrette sauce (see below) and season to taste.
- Pour some vinaigrette sauce on to the lettuce leaves and the blanched beans and arrange carefully on a plate.
- Arrange the goose livers, chanterelles, mushrooms and watercress attractively in the middle of the plate.

Sauce vinaigrette

10g	(½oz)	shallots, finely chopped
5cl	(2fl oz)	red wine vinegar
10cl	(4fl oz)	walnut oil
1g		chives, chopped
		a little lemon juice
		salt, freshly ground pepper

▶

Method

- Reduce the red wine vinegar, with the shallots, to half the original volume and leave to cool.
- Gradually work in the walnut oil.
- Add the chives.
- Season with lemon juice, salt and pepper.

Note It is important that the goose livers, chanterelles and mushrooms are sautéd at the last minute so that they may be served warm.

Salade aux huîtres Catherine
Oyster salad with spinach

Ingredients (for 4 people)

24		medium sized oysters
5cl	(2fl oz)	dry white wine
2g		finely chopped shallot
2		medium sized courgettes
2		medium sized carrots
		a little sugar
80g	(3¼oz)	young spinach, blanched
		salt, freshly ground pepper
		sauce vinaigrette (see below)
		finely chopped chives

Method (See Plate 7)

- Scrub the oysters under running water, then open.
- Take them out of their shells with a knife and remove the beard.
- Reduce the white wine and shallots to half the original volume and add the oysters.
- Bring to the boil quickly, put the oysters on ice and allow to cool in the stock.
- Remove the oysters to a plate and reduce the stock again.

▶

- Hollow out the courgettes with an apple corer.
- Boil up quickly in salted water and cool immediately.
- Boil the carrots until crisp in salted water and a little sugar, then allow to cool in their own water.
- Stuff the courgettes with the trimmed carrots and then slice.
- Arrange the spinach attractively on a plate, season the oysters and sprinkle with vinaigrette, then place on top.
- Garnish with the courgettes and carrots.
- Sprinkle with finely chopped chives.

Sauce vinaigrette

2g		Dijon mustard
5cl	(2fl oz)	Sherry vinegar
10cl	(4fl oz)	olive oil
		reduced oyster stock (see above)
		salt, freshly ground pepper

Method
- Mix all the above ingredients together, stirring constantly and season to taste.

Note It is important that the courgettes and carrots are allowed to cool in the water in which they have been blanched. The oysters should only just be brought to the boil, otherwise they will lose too much flavour.

‘We chefs are continually seeking to improve the taste and nutritional value of our cooking to the highest standard and are therefore striving to make dishes lighter and more easily digestible. The art of cooking must be raised to the level of science without undermining its artistic character and its recipes, which are often still too complicated, must be subjected to a precise method which excludes all uncertainty. ’

Salade d'avocats
Avocado salad with mushrooms

Ingredients (for 4 people)

4		halves of well ripened avocados, cut into thin slices
150g	(5oz)	peeled tomatoes, diced
200g	(7oz)	mushrooms, raw and cut into fine slices
150g	(5oz)	green salad (lettuce, endive)

Method
- Season the avocados, diced tomatoes, mushrooms and salad and arrange attractively on a plate. Serve with the following sauce.

Sauce

20g	(¾oz)	Dijon mustard
5cl	(2fl oz)	red wine vinegar
15cl	(¼ pint)	walnut oil
		salt
		lemon juice
		finely chopped herbs

Method
- Mix the mustard, wine vinegar and walnut oil. Season with salt, lemon juice and finely chopped herbs.

Note The herbs may be varied depending on the season but basil, chervil and chives are most suitable.

Rosette de saumon fumé à la mousse de truite Dorchester

Smoked salmon with trout mousse Dorchester-style

This recipe was created in the Dorchester Hotel. To make the service easier for the waiter, we arranged the smoked salmon in individual glass dishes, stuffed with the trout mousse, turned out and garnished. This dish can be prepared in exactly the same way for more than just 4 people. A great success!

Ingredients (for 4 people)

8		slices of Scottish smoked salmon, finely cut
120g	(4½oz)	smoked trout fillet
2		leaves of gelatine, soaked in cold water and dissolved in 2cl (¾fl oz) of warm water
20cl	(6fl oz)	whipped cream
2cl	(¾fl oz)	Sherry
1cl	(½fl oz)	Cognac
		some fresh horseradish, finely grated
		salt, freshly ground pepper

Garnish

4	lettuce leaves
4	red chicory leaves
4	half slices of cucumber
4	slices of hard-boiled egg
4	tomato slices
4	slices of truffle
4	sprigs of parsley

▶

Method (See Plate 6)
- Arrange the finely cut slices of salmon in small glass dishes to overlap the sides. Place in the refrigerator.
- Purée the smoked trout fillet.
- Add the dissolved gelatine with the water.
- Carefully work in the whipped cream.
- Add the Sherry and Cognac.
- Season with the finely grated horseradish, salt and pepper.
- Put this carefully made mousse into the glass dishes.
- Fold the salmon sides back over the mousse.
- Allow to rest for about half an hour in the refrigerator.
- Turn out on to a plate decorated with the lettuce and red chicory leaves.
- Garnish with the slices of cucumber, egg, tomato, truffles and sprigs of parsley.

Note Pieces of smoked salmon may be used instead of smoked trout fillet. Slices of brown bread should be served with this mousse.

Loup de mer cru aux oeufs de homard
Raw sea bass with lobster eggs

Ingredients (for 4 people)

1		fresh sea bass (750-850g (1½-1¾lb))
6cl	(2½fl oz)	cold pressed olive oil, from the first press
		salt, freshly ground pepper
		a few poached lobster eggs
		a few finely plucked chervil leaves

Hors
d'oeuvre

Method

- Carefully gut the sea bass, without washing or scaling it.
- Take off the fillets, and remove all the bones.
- Coat lightly with olive oil and allow to rest in the refrigerator for about 1 hour (to tenderise the fish).
- Cut the fillets into very thin slices and arrange attractively on a plate.
- Coat with olive oil, season with salt and freshly ground pepper.
- Poach the lobster eggs lightly in salted water, dry and arrange on the fish with the chervil.

Note It is of the utmost importance that only the very freshest produce is used. French bread freshly toasted, served hot, makes a good accompaniment to this dish.

Terrine Covent Garden
Vegetable terrine Covent Garden

Ingredients (for 10 people)

2		globe artichokes
20g	(¾oz)	veal kidney fat (for cooking artichoke)
40g	(1½oz)	mange-tout, stringed and blanched for 4 seconds
80g	(3¼oz)	green beans, stringed and blanched quickly
400g	(14oz)	broccoli, cleaned and blanched quickly
350g	(12oz)	small carrots, peeled, blanched and cut into quarters lengthwise
200g	(7oz)	small courgettes, blanched and cut into quarters lengthwise

▶

100g	(4oz)	small chanterelles, cleaned and blanched.
10g	(½oz)	butter
		salt, freshly ground pepper
1		tomato cut into quarters and watercress to garnish

Method (See Plate 6)
- Break off the stems of the artichokes and cut away three quarters of the leafy head with a knife.
- Remove the remaining leaves from the artichoke bottoms and take out the inside choke of the artichokes by means of a small Parisienne cutter.
- Blanch the bottoms immediately in salted water, some lemon juice and a little olive oil (see page 256).
- Now cook the artichoke bottoms in more salted water and veal kidney fat until crisp.
- Allow to cool in the stock and cut into slices.
- Butter a terrine dish, mix together one third of the chicken farce and the watercress purée (see recipe 45) and place on the bottom of the dish.
- Fill the terrine dish with a layer of each of the pre-blanched vegetables, spreading some chicken farce between each layer of vegetable. Season to taste.
- Cover and poach for about 35 minutes in a bain-marie in a moderate oven.
- Allow to cool and cut into not too thin slices.
- Arrange on tomato vinaigrette (see recipe 46) and garnish with tomato quarters and watercress.

Note When arranging the vegetables in the terrine it is advisable to place them so that the colours look attractive when the terrine is cut.

Farce de volaille
Chicken forcemeat

Ingredients (for 10 people)

80g	(3¼oz)	white chicken meat (breast without skin)
20cl	(6fl oz)	double cream
75g	(3oz)	watercress, with stalks removed salt, freshly ground pepper

Method
- Remove the sinew from the meat and mince finely, then press through a sieve.
- Put in a bowl on ice and allow to cool well.
- Mix in the cream a little at a time until a light, airy farce is formed.
- Liquidise the watercress with a little white poultry stock (see recipe 1).
- Mix a third of the farce with the watercress purée.
- Season both farces with salt and pepper.

Note It is important that the vegetables are allowed to cool in the water in which they were blanched and this should be cooled on ice. Only in this way is the individual taste of each vegetable brought out. It goes without saying that all the vegetables used here must remain crisp.

Sauce vinaigrette à la tomate
Tomato vinaigrette

Ingredients (for 10 people)

20cl	(6fl oz)	chicken stock greatly reduced (see recipe 1)
20g	(¾oz)	tomato purée
100g	(4oz)	ripe tomatoes
5cl	(2fl oz)	red wine vinegar
5cl	(2fl oz)	olive oil
		salt, freshly ground pepper
		a little sugar and lemon juice (optional)

Method
- Mix the chicken stock with the tomato purée.
- Liquidise the fresh tomatoes and add to the above mixture with the vinegar.
- Add the olive oil very gradually, season with salt and freshly ground pepper and, if necessary, a little sugar and lemon juice.

6 Cooking should bring out and improve the natural tastes and emphasise them with garnishes and sauces which are chosen to harmonise. 9

Terrine de hareng à l'aneth
Herring terrine with dill

Ingredients (for 10 people)

250g	(9oz)	pike
150g	(5oz)	smoked bacon, blanched without rind
30cl	(½ pint)	double cream
2g		finely chopped dill
		a little sweet paprika
15		crayfish tails, freshly poached
150g	(5oz)	barding lard
300g	(10oz)	herring fillets
		salt, freshly ground pepper, dill

Method

- Trim the pike well, salt and mince with the smoked bacon, if necessary passing through a fine sieve afterwards.
- Place on ice and gradually mix in the cream.
- Mix one half of the pike farce with the chopped dill and the other with paprika and the freshly poached crayfish tails.
- Line a terrine dish with barding lard and put in dill and crayfish tail farce to a depth of 1cm (½in).
- Put in a layer of herring fillets, carefully trimmed, and cover with dill.
- Put a layer of paprika and crayfish tail farce on top and again garnish with dill.
- Put in a second layer of herring fillets and cover with the rest of the crayfish tail farce.
- Cover with barding lard and poach in the oven in a bain-marie for about 30 minutes at approximately 150°C (300°F).

Terrine de ris de veau et de volaille
Terrine of sweetbreads and chicken

Ingredients (for 10 people)

280g	(9½oz)	sweetbreads, soaked until clean
0cl	(3fl oz)	Cognac
15cl	(¼ pint)	Port
20g	(¾oz)	shallots, finely chopped
		a few parsley stalks
		thyme, bay leaf
40g	(1½oz)	butter
170g	(6oz)	pork ⎫
170g	(6oz)	veal ⎬ well trimmed
135g	(4¾oz)	chicken ⎭
120g	(4½oz)	goose liver
40cl	(¾ pint)	double cream
25g	(1oz)	pistachio nuts
15g	(½oz)	liquid meat extract (see recipe 9)
		salt, freshly ground pepper
130g	(4½oz)	barding lard

Method

- Trim the sweetbreads and cut in half.
- Marinate them in the Cognac and Port with chopped shallots, thyme, bay leaf and parsley stalks.
- Sauté in butter until lightly browned.
- Add the marinade and simmer for 5 minutes.
- Remove the sweetbreads and skin, reduce the stock to a glaze.
- Add the cream, pistachio nuts and the meat extract and season well.
- Line a terrine dish with the barding lard and half fill with the farce.
- Press in the sweetbreads and fill with the rest of the farce. ▶

- Cover with lard and lay thyme leaves on top.
- Cover and poach in a bain-marie in the oven for about 35 minutes at 150°C (300°F).

Note Chicken livers may be used instead of goose livers but these must first be marinated in milk.

Terrine de foie de canard
Duck liver terrine

Ingredients (for 10 people)

3		raw duck livers (400g (14oz) each)
50cl	(18fl oz)	milk
10g	(½oz)	salt
3.5g		spice mixture (see recipe 50)
		a little sugar
3cl	(1fl oz)	Port
3cl	(1fl oz)	good Cognac
180g	(6oz)	unsalted fresh bacon/barding lard
1		bay leaf

Method
- Carefully separate the livers (taking the larger part away from the smaller part).
- Cut the gall bladder out of the liver with a knife.
- Sometimes the liver is of a greenish colour around the gall bladder—remove this also, otherwise the terrine will have a bitter after-taste.
- Remove the fine thin skin which covers the liver.
- Carefully remove the nerves. To do this, cut deeply into one half of the liver and, with a knife and your thumb, take hold of the nerve which begins at the top of the liver and pull it slowly downward, thereby removing it. ▶

- When the liver has been cleaned in this manner, it should be laid in the salted milk, covered and allowed to stand in the refrigerator for 12 hours.
- Remove the liver and dry in a cloth.
- Mix the spice mixture, sugar, a little salt, the Port and Cognac together in a bowl.
- Add the liver, cover with aluminium foil and marinate in the refrigerator for 12 hours.
- The livers should be frequently turned during this time.
- Line a terrine mould with thin slices of bacon or barding lard.
- Remove the livers from the marinade and place carefully in the terrine mould.
- Any holes should be smoothed over, using a soup spoon.
- Lay the smaller part of the liver on top and smooth over.
- There should be no holes or gaps left in the mixture.
- Cover with barding lard, place a bay leaf on top and poach carefully in a bain-marie for about 45 to 50 minutes.
- Remove the poached terrine from the oven and allow to cool in the bain-marie with a small weight on it.
- When completely cooled remove the terrine, wash the mould thoroughly, place any fat that has run out in a saucepan and melt.
- Return the well trimmed terrine to the mould, pour the melted fat over it and store in the refrigerator.

Note It is important that the water in the bain-marie is kept at 70°-75°C (158°-167°F), otherwise the liver will lose too much fat.

Mélange d'épices pour foie gras

Mixed spices for goose or duck terrine

Ingredients

35g	(1¼oz)	ground nutmeg
35g	(1¼oz)	cloves
10g	(½oz)	bay leaves
20g	(¾oz)	white pepper
10g	(½oz)	black pepper
20g	(¾oz)	cinnamon
10g	(½oz)	ginger
5g	(¼oz)	cardamom
10g	(½oz)	marjoram
20g	(¾oz)	coriander
10g	(½oz)	basil
30g	(1¼oz)	mace
10g	(½oz)	thyme
10g	(½oz)	juniper berries
5g	(¼oz)	curry powder
10g	(½oz)	tarragon
5g	(¼oz)	chervil
5g	(¼oz)	rosemary
5g	(¼oz)	pepper leaves
2g	pinch	cayenne
5g	(¼oz)	dill
3g	pinch	ground fennel

Method

- Grind up finely all the ingredients.
- Use 5g (¼oz) per 1kg (2lb) foie gras.

Parfait de foies de volaille aux truffes

Chicken liver parfait with truffles

Ingredients (for 10 people)

250g	(9oz)	poultry liver
50g	(2oz)	goose liver trimmings from terrine de foie de canard (see recipe 49)
		salt, freshly ground pepper
200g	(7oz)	butter
2cl	(¾fl oz)	truffle stock (juice from bottled truffles)
2cl	(¾fl oz)	Sherry
1cl	(½fl oz)	Cognac
5g	(¼oz)	chopped truffle
10cl	(4fl oz)	whipped cream
		a little sugar

Method

- Clean the livers well, remove the nerves and gall bladders.
- Heat the butter in a saucepan.
- Place the poultry liver in the melted butter, season with salt and pepper and cook carefully for about 15 minutes. Leave to cool.
- Mince the cooled livers with the butter and goose liver and finally press through a fine hair sieve.
- Place the mousse on ice and flavour with the truffle stock, Sherry, Cognac and chopped truffle.
- Carefully work in the whipped cream with a wooden spoon.
- Season with salt, pepper and a pinch of sugar.
- Allow the mousse to harden a little, cut out mussel shapes with a spoon and garnish accordingly.

Note Make sure that when combining the mousse and the whipped cream, they are both at the same temperature.

Poésie de cuisses de grenouilles au Riesling
Frogs' legs in puff pastry

Ingredients (for 4 people)

24		frogs' legs
5g	(¼oz)	finely chopped shallot
		a little finely chopped garlic
20g	(¾oz)	butter
8		grains of saffron
10cl	(4fl oz)	white wine (Riesling)
15cl	(¼ pint)	white veal stock (see recipe 2)
		juice of half a lemon
10cl	(4fl oz)	double cream
40g	(1½oz)	butter to finish the sauce
		a few chives, finely cut
		salt, freshly ground pepper
4		rectangles of puff pastry, approximately 8 × 5cm (3¼ × 2in) (see recipe 19)
200g	(7oz)	young spinach, stalks removed and blanched
20g	(¾oz)	butter, to sauté the spinach

Method

- Season the frogs' legs with salt and pepper.
- Sweat the shallots and garlic in butter and add the frogs' legs with the saffron.
- Add the Riesling.
- Put in the veal stock and lemon juice and carefully simmer the frogs' legs until cooked. Leave to cool in the stock.
- Remove the meat from the bones and reduce the stock.
- Add the cream and reduce until the required consistency is achieved.
- Monté with butter.

▶

- Add the meat and chives and season to taste with salt and pepper.
- Meanwhile carefully bake the puff pastry.
- Sauté the spinach in butter.
- Cut the top off each puff pastry rectangle, fill the lower half with the sautéd and well seasoned spinach and place the frogs' legs ragoût on top.
- Finish with the pastry top on each.

Tourte aux écrevisses
Crayfish tart

Ingredients (for 4 people)

250g	(9oz)	shortcrust pastry (see recipe 18)
16		freshwater crayfish
		court-bouillon (see recipe 7)
250g	(9oz)	young spinach, blanched
25cl	(9fl oz)	egg mixture (see below)
1		egg white
		salt, freshly ground pepper
3cl	(1¼fl oz)	whipped cream
5cl	(2fl oz)	crayfish sauce (see recipe 24)

Method
- Roll out the pastry and line a cake tin with it, allowing it to stand up at the edges.
- Prick the pastry with a fork and keep cool until needed.
- Wash the crayfish well, place in boiling court-bouillon and allow to simmer for 2 minutes.
- Remove the crayfish, break open and remove the stomach.
- Chop the spinach coarsely and mix with the egg mixture.
- Put the mixture into the cake tin until two thirds full.
- Bake in a pre-heated oven for about 20 to 25 minutes at 180°-200°C (350°-400°F).   ▶

- Arrange the warm and well seasoned crayfish tails and claws on top.
- Mix the cream with the crayfish sauce, pour sparingly over the cake and, just before serving, brown it a little under the grill.

Egg mixture

3		eggs
		some cornflour
10cl	(4fl oz)	double cream
		salt, nutmeg, freshly ground pepper

Method

- Mix the eggs, cornflour and double cream together in a liquidiser.
- Season with salt, pepper and nutmeg.

‘ Before the culinary revolution at the beginning of this century nearly all restaurants offered the same dishes on their menus. The customers ordered only those dishes with which they were acquainted. The main problem of today's grande cuisine is not its definition, whether new or classical, but rather the provision of natural foodstuffs, because where chemistry triumphs the chef is irrecoverably lost. Oysters from industrial waters, deep frozen scallops, chickens from the conveyor belt, drug-fed calves, sprayed vegetables, cheese which has been spoilt in refrigerated vehicles and watered down wines herald the end of the art of cooking. Whereas in Escoffier's time no pollution damaged natural products, head chefs today have to devote time and a special resourcefulness to the provision of their raw materials. Today we look for farmers who fatten their pigs with chestnuts, go ourselves earlier to the market and have fresh products flown in by air in order to spoil the gourmets according to Escoffier's rules, with smaller portions and more wholesome ingredients. ’

PLATE 6
Above: Terrine Covent Garden. Vegetable terrine Covent Garden *(Recipe 44).*

Left: Rosette de Saumon fumé au mousse de truite Dorchester. Smoked salmon with trout mousse Dorchester-style *(Recipe 42).*

PLATE 5 *(Previous page)*
Méli-mélo de homard aux pointes d'asperges. Lobster salad with asparagus *(Recipe 37).*

Médaillons de foie gras au vin rouge
Fresh goose liver with red wine and shallots

This is something different. Why should goose liver always be served cold? As long as the foie gras is absolutely fresh, one can create wonderful dishes with it.

Ingredients (for 4 people)

240g	(8½oz)	raw goose liver
		salt, freshly ground pepper
10cl	(4fl oz)	red wine
2.5cl	(1fl oz)	red wine vinegar
20g	(¾oz)	shallots, chopped
10cl	(4fl oz)	walnut oil
10g	(½oz)	chives, finely cut
		a little lemon juice

Method

- Remove skin and nerves from the goose liver with a knife (see recipe 49).
- Cut into slices approximately 1cm (½in) thick.
- Season the goose liver and sauté on both sides briefly in a hot pan without fat.
- Arrange on a warm plate.
- To make the sauce, reduce the red wine and red wine vinegar with the shallots to half their original volume and leave to cool slightly.
- Gradually stir in the walnut oil, add a little chives and lemon juice. Add salt and pepper according to taste.
- Pour over the liver and cover with chives.

Note It is important that the goose liver be served pink.

Ravioli alla Casalinga
Homemade ravioli with mushrooms and tomatoes

This is a typical recipe which we prepared in Rome, superb in taste and well presented. Whenever I hear or read the word ravioli, I can smell the fresh herbs and remember wonderful Italy.

Ravioli paste (see recipe 21)

Filling ingredients (for 10 people)

10g	(¼oz)	finely chopped shallots
20g	(¾oz)	butter
150g	(5oz)	veal (leg)
150g	(5oz)	pork (neck), cut into cubes
50g	(2oz)	salami or raw ham
		a little sage, rosemary and basil
50g	(2oz)	tomatoes, diced
10cl	(4fl oz)	white wine
30cl	(½ pint)	brown veal stock (see recipe 4)
100g	(4oz)	spinach, blanched
50g	(2oz)	veal brain, soaked and cleaned
1		egg yolk
30g	(1¼oz)	Parmesan cheese, freshly grated
30g	(1¼oz)	butter
5		small sage leaves
		salt, freshly ground pepper

Garnish

30g	(1¼oz)	Parmesan cheese, freshly grated
30g	(1¼oz)	butter
5		sage leaves } to finish
		salt, freshly ground pepper

Method for the filling
- Sweat the shallots in butter, add the well trimmed veal and pork and sweat well.
- Add the salami or raw ham and the herbs.
- Add the tomatoes and white wine and reduce. ▶

- Add the veal stock and braise until tender.
- Add the spinach and mix in well.
- Add the blanched veal brain, bind with the egg yolk and pass through a fine sieve.
- Mix in the Parmesan cheese.
- Strain a little brown butter to which the sage leaves (cut in halves) have been added and mix in.
- Season with salt and pepper.

Method for the ravioli

- Cut the ravioli paste into two equal pieces, roll out thinly, mark one half with a round pastry cutter and brush with egg.
- Put some filling, about 2-3mm (⅛in) thick, on to each circle.
- Lay the other half of the paste on top and press lightly.
- Cut the ravioli with a ravioli cutter into even squares.
- Cook the ravioli for 5-8 minutes in plenty of salted water to which a little oil has been added to prevent the ravioli from sticking together.
- Drain, sauté in butter and season.
- Put some of the sauce into a suitable dish, add the ravioli and pour some more sauce over it.
- Sprinkle with freshly grated Parmesan cheese and brown under the grill or in a hot oven.
- Warm some butter with sage leaves until brown, strain, pour over the ravioli and serve immediately.

Sauce

3g		finely chopped shallot
20g	(¾oz)	butter
50g	(2oz)	mushrooms, sliced
50g	(2oz)	tomatoes, diced
5cl	(2fl oz)	white wine
30cl	(½ pint)	brown veal stock (see recipe 4)
		salt, freshly ground pepper

Method

- Sweat the shallots in butter, add the mushrooms and sweat.
- Add the diced tomatoes and white wine and reduce.
- Add the brown veal stock and season to taste.

Coquilles St. Jacques galloises
Scallops fried in butter with leeks

Ingredients (for 4 people)

8		large scallops in their shells (approximately 240g (8½oz) net)
200g	(7oz)	green leeks
5cl	(2fl oz)	dry white wine
2.5cl	(1fl oz)	water
		salt, freshly ground pepper
10cl	(4fl oz)	double cream
20g	(¾oz)	butter
4		fresh basil leaves, roe for garnish

Method (See Plate 11)

- Prepare the scallops as for Rendez-vous de Fruits-de-mer (**see recipe 104**).
- Cut the leeks into pieces and wash well.
- Cook the leeks in white wine, water, salt and pepper.
- Liquidise, bring to the boil with the cream and reduce.
- Finish with butter.
- Dry the scallops, season them and quickly sauté in butter until golden brown.
- Arrange the leek purée in a suitable dish with the scallops on top.
- Sprinkle with a little brown butter, to which at, the last minute, the basil leaves have been added.
- Serve with some roe and a basil leaf as garnish.

Note It is an attractive idea to serve the scallops in their shells on lightly coloured sea salt (see photograph).

Mousseline de coquilles St. Jacques
Mousseline of scallops with fresh tomato purée

Many ideas occur to me at Billingsgate fish market in London, such as this very simple but effective dish. As you are strolling through the market in the morning you automatically start to create and combine ingredients.

Ingredients (for 4 people)

6		large scallops in their shells (approximately 180g (6oz) net)
80g	(3¼oz)	pike, without skin salt, freshly ground pepper, a little cayenne
25cl	(9fl oz)	double cream

Garnish

20g	(¾oz)	fresh tomato purée
4		truffle slices, finely cut
4		puff pastry fleurons (see recipe 19)

Method (See Plate 9)

- Open the scallops, remove the skin, wash well and dry on a cloth.
- Finely mince five of the scallops with the roes and the well trimmed pike. Allow to cool in a bowl on ice.
- Season with salt, pepper and a little cayenne and gradually mix in the cream.
- Press the mixture through a hair sieve, season again and keep cool.
- Cut one of the scallops into small cubes, season with salt and pepper and add to the mousseline as garnish.
- Put the mousseline into small moulds, tapping them hard so that the air is allowed to escape.
- Poach in a bain-marie in the oven for approximately 15 minutes.

▶

- Allow to rest for three to four minutes before serving so that the mousseline comes away from the mould easily.
- Arrange on a plate and cover with the following sauce.

Sauce

5cl	(2fl oz)	Noilly Prat
10cl	(4fl oz)	fish stock (see recipe 6)
5g	(¼oz)	finely chopped shallot
20cl	(6fl oz)	double cream
60g	(2½oz)	butter, to finish
		salt, freshly ground pepper

Method

- Reduce the Noilly Prat and fish stock together with the finely chopped shallot, add the cream and reduce to the required consistency.
- Strain through a fine sieve or muslin and monté with butter.
- Season with salt and pepper.
- Cover the mousseline with this sauce.
- Garnish with the tomato purée, slices of truffle and the fleurons.

Dublin Bay prawns
Maître Gilgen

Mr. Gilgen, a true expert, has been head chef for many years in the Kulm Hotel in St. Moritz. I had the opportunity to spend three very instructive and happy seasons there. The gourmets amongst the guests usually preferred this dish for lunch.

Ingredients (for 4 people)

24		pieces of scampi (or 320g (11oz)) net without shells)
		salt, freshly ground pepper, cayenne
30g	(1¼oz)	butter
		fresh tarragon, dill and parsley, finely chopped
20cl	(6fl oz)	white wine
20cl	(6fl oz)	hollandaise sauce (see recipe 26)
5cl	(2fl oz)	whipped cream
10cl	(4fl oz)	natural yoghurt
5g	(¼oz)	freshly ground horseradish
2		lettuce hearts, cut into strips
		a little lemon juice
4		pieces of toast

Method
- Sweat the seasoned scampi in butter.
- Add the chopped herbs and white wine.
- Bring to the boil, cover and simmer for 15 seconds.
- Remove the scampi and reduce the stock.
- Add the hollandaise sauce and whipped cream to the cooled stock and taste.
- Mix the yoghurt and horseradish with the lettuce and flavour with lemon juice, salt, pepper and cayenne.
- Pour on to the warm pieces of toast, and arrange the scampi on top.
- Cover with the sauce and glaze under the grill.

Note So that the toast remains crisp, it is advisable to prepare this dish at the last minute.

Huîtres moscovite au Champagne

Oysters with Champagne sauce and caviar

Ingredients (for 4 people)

24		Belon oysters
20cl	(6fl oz)	Champagne
30cl	(½ pint)	double cream
1		egg yolk
		salt, freshly ground white pepper, cayenne
20g	(¾oz)	caviar

Method

- Open the oysters, take out the flesh and remove the beard (keep the oyster water).
- Poach the oysters briefly in the Champagne and oyster water.
- Remove the oysters and place in the warmed shells.
- Reduce the stock, add the cream and reduce until the required consistency is achieved.
- Remove from the heat and stir the egg yolk into the sauce.
- Season with salt, pepper and cayenne.
- Cover the oysters with the sauce and glaze under the grill.
- Arrange the caviar on top and serve immediately.

Note The oysters may be arranged attractively on a plate with coarse sea salt.

Chapter 4

Soups

Potage de légumes froid
Cold vegetable soup with basil

Ingredients (for 4 people)

200g	(7oz)	peeled tomatoes, coarsely chopped
100g	(4oz)	peeled cucumber, cut into small pieces
30g	(1¼oz)	onion, finely chopped
30g	(1¼oz)	red and green peppers, with core removed and coarsely chopped some finely chopped garlic
15g	(½oz)	white breadcrumbs
2cl	(¾fl oz)	red wine vinegar
5cl	(2fl oz)	poultry stock, without fat, (see recipe 1)
4cl	(1½fl oz)	olive oil some oregano and 6 basil leaves
5cl	(2fl oz)	single cream salt, freshly ground pepper

Method

- Mix together the tomatoes, cucumber, onion, peppers, garlic and breadcrumbs.
- Add the vinegar, poultry stock, olive oil, oregano and 3 basil leaves.
- Season with salt and pepper.
- Marinate for 12 hours.
- Liquidise to make a fine purée and strain through a sieve.
- Finish with the cream and season again.
- Add the remaining basil leaves cut in thin strips.
- Keep cold.

Note It is important that this soup is served very cold (possibly on ice).

Elixir de cailles aux oeufs
Clear quail soup with soft eggs

Ingredients (for 4 people)

400g	(14oz)	quail bones, stomach and skin
½		veal knuckle
3cl	(1fl oz)	peanut oil
1.5 litres	(2½ pints)	water
		salt
40g	(1½oz)	onion, with skins
1		clove
½		bay leaf
20g	(¾oz)	carrot
40g	(1½oz)	leek
40g	(1½oz)	celery

To clarify

200g	(7oz)	raw quail and poultry meat, coarsely minced
2		egg whites
50g	(2oz)	tomatoes, coarsely cut
50g	(2oz)	celery
5g	(¼oz)	parsley stalks
		a few tarragon stalks
10cl	(4fl oz)	dry white wine
		salt, freshly ground pepper

Garnish

10g	(½oz)	celery ⎫ cut into julienne
10g	(½oz)	leek ⎬ strips (see page 295)
10g	(½oz)	carrot ⎭ and blanched
4		quails' eggs, boiled for 3 minutes and carefully shelled
		a few sprigs watercress, with stalks carefully removed

▶

Method (See Plate 9)

- Carefully sauté the quail bones, stomach and skin and veal knuckle, in the peanut oil.
- Place everything, without the cooking fat, in a saucepan, add the water, salt sparingly and bring to the boil.
- Skim and allow to simmer for 45 minutes.
- Colour the onion, garnished with the clove and bay leaf, directly on the top of the stove, add to the stock and then simmer for a further 30 minutes with the carrot, leek and celery.
- Pass through a sieve and allow to cool.

Clarifying the stock

- Mix the quail and poultry meat well with the egg whites, tomatoes, celery and stalks of parsley and tarragon.
- Add the stock and white wine.
- Bring to the boil while stirring constantly and then allow to simmer for 20 minutes.
- Season with salt and pepper.
- Pass through a fine muslin sieve and remove the fat.
- Put the elixir into cups.
- Garnish with the prepared vegetables and the quails' eggs.
- Add the watercress and serve immediately.

Note This soup was one of our greatest successes at the World Exhibition 1970 in Osaka, Japan, where I was employed as head chef. A simple concentrated clear soup which we covered with pastry and then baked in the oven *à la minute*. When you cover the soup with pastry, you must be careful that the quails' eggs remain soft although they are baked in the oven for 12-13 minutes. They should be boiled for a very short time and then carefully shelled.

Potage aux quenelles de foie
Double consommé with liver quenelles

Ingredients (for 4 people)

50g	(2oz)	veal liver, well trimmed
50g	(2oz)	beef liver, well trimmed
2		bread rolls
10cl	(4fl oz)	milk, for soaking the rolls
20g	(¾oz)	onion, finely chopped and sautéd in butter
60g	(2½oz)	veal kidney fat, chopped and mixed with a little flour
1		egg
		salt, freshly ground pepper
		a little marjoram, rosemary and sage
		a little sugar
80cl	(1¼ pints)	meat broth (see recipe 11)
8		slices of marrow, blanched
		a little parsley, coarsely chopped

Method

- Mince the liver, soaked rolls, onion and veal kidney fat, but not too finely.
- Mix all these together in a bowl on ice, work in the egg and season with salt, pepper, herbs and a little sugar.
- Make small dumplings with a spoon and poach carefully in the broth for 3 to 4 minutes.
- Serve the liver dumplings in the well seasoned beef stock with the blanched slices of marrow and the chopped parsley.

Scotch broth

Ingredients (for 4 people)

20g	(¾oz)	onion, finely chopped
20g	(¾oz)	butter
30g	(1¼oz)	carrot, diced
30g	(1¼oz)	leek, cut into small cubes
20g	(¾oz)	celeriac, cut into small cubes
20g	(¾oz)	cabbage, cut into cubes
30g	(1¼oz)	pearl barley
1 litre	(1¾ pints)	lamb stock
50g	(2oz)	boiled lamb, cut into cubes (see note)
		salt, freshly ground pepper
		chopped parsley

Method

- Sweat the onions in the butter.
- Add the carrot, leek and celeriac and sweat well, add the cabbage and the thoroughly washed barley.
- Add the lamb stock and bring to the boil.
- Add the lamb just before serving, season to taste with salt and pepper.

Note For this recipe the lamb should be boiled in advance. It is a good idea to boil it separately so that both the meat and the stock can be used.

❛ The whole secret of successful cooking — more, the very essence of culinary perfection — is, or should be, simplicity. ❜

Potage aux chanterelles
Chanterelle soup

Ingredients (for 4 people)

5g	(¼oz)	finely chopped shallot
1g		finely chopped garlic
2cl	(¾fl oz)	olive oil
300g	(10oz)	chanterelles, carefully cleaned
50cl	(18fl oz)	vegetable stock (see recipe 13)
20cl	(6fl oz)	double cream
		salt, nutmeg and freshly ground pepper
		a little lemon juice
		thyme leaves to garnish

Method

- Carefully sweat the shallot and garlic in olive oil
- Add the finely chopped chanterelles and sweat quickly.
- Add the vegetable stock and allow to simmer for 3-4 minutes.
- Liquidise the mixture, bring to the boil again and finish with the cream.
- Season with salt, nutmeg, pepper and lemon juice.
- When serving, garnish with thyme leaves.

Note Small chanterelles may also be served in this very delicate soup.

PLATE 7
Above: Salade aux huîtres Catherine. Oyster salad with spinach *(Recipe 40).*

Left: Rendez-vous de fruits-de-mer à la crème de basilic. Seafood in basil sauce *(Recipe 104).*

PLATE 8 *(Overleaf)*
Billy Bye soup *(Recipe 68).*

Potage Pigalle
Leek soup with white wine

Ingredients (for 4 people)

200g	(7oz)	onions, finely chopped
200g	(7oz)	leeks, finely chopped
40g	(1½oz)	butter
10cl	(4fl oz)	white wine
10cl	(4fl oz)	brown veal stock (see recipe 4)
60cl	(1 pint)	meat broth (see recipe 11)
		salt, freshly ground pepper
		a little coarsely chopped parsley

Method

- Sweat the onions and leeks carefully in butter until golden.
- Add the white wine and brown veal stock and reduce a little.
- Add the broth and allow to simmer for 8-10 minutes.
- Season with salt and pepper and garnish with the parsley before serving.

Potage aux escargots
Snail soup with vermouth

Ingredients (for 4 people)

24		fresh snails
30cl	(11fl oz)	consommé, reduced (see recipe 11)
20g	(¾oz)	leek ⎫
20g	(¾oz)	celery ⎬ cut into strips
20g	(¾oz)	carrot ⎭
10g	(½oz)	butter
50cl	(18fl oz)	white veal stock (see recipe 2)
20cl	(6fl oz)	double cream
1		egg yolk
2cl	(¾fl oz)	Noilly Prat
		salt, freshly ground pepper
		a few fennel leaves, finely chopped

Method

- Prepare the snails (see recipe 67) then marinate them in the concentrated consommé.
- Sweat the leek, celery and carrots in butter and add the snails.
- Add the consommé and reduce.
- Add the white veal stock and allow to simmer for 5 minutes.
- Mix the cream with the egg yolk and Noilly Prat and add to the soup.
- Bring to the boil and season with salt and pepper.
- Arrange in a suitable dish and garnish with finely chopped fennel leaves.

Préparation des escargots
Preparation of snails

Ingredients (for 60 snails)

60		snails
50g	(2oz)	finely chopped onions
30g	(1¼oz)	carrots
50g	(2oz)	leek, just the white part
30g	(1¼oz)	celery
40g	(1½oz)	butter
		a little thyme, rosemary, basil
		a small amount of garlic
10cl	(4fl oz)	dry white wine
1 litre	(1¾ pints)	poultry stock (see recipe 1)
1		small knuckle of veal, cut into cubes
		salt, freshly ground pepper

(carrots, leek, celery) } diced

Method

- Only closed snails should be used.
- Remove the calcium operculum (the membrane covering of the opening) with the tip of a knife.
- Wash the snails several times and leave them in heavily salted water for 2½ hours to remove the mud and dirt.
- Put the snails in a saucepan, fill with water, bring to the boil and allow to drain immediately.
- Remove the snails from their shells with the help of a pin and then remove the black part at the end of the snail.
- Sweat the onions, carrots, leek and celery in butter.
- Add the herbs and garlic and continue to sweat.
- Add the white wine, reduce and add the poultry stock.
- Add the snails and the knuckle of veal and allow to stew for about 3 hours.
- Season with salt and pepper and store the snails in this stock until needed.

Billy Bye soup

Ingredients (for 4 people)

1kg	(2lb)	mussels
10g	(½oz)	finely chopped shallot
20g	(¾oz)	finely chopped onion
		a few sprigs of parsley and dill
¼		bay leaf
10cl	(4fl oz)	dry white wine
50g	(2oz)	celery and carrots cut in julienne strips
20g	(¾oz)	butter
50cl	(18fl oz)	fish stock (see recipe 6)
20cl	(6fl oz)	double cream
1		egg yolk mixed with a little cream
		a little curry powder, salt,
		freshly ground pepper
4		truffle slices, cut into julienne strips
		a little plucked chervil

Method (See Plate 8)

- Scrape the mussels clean, brush them, and wash thoroughly.
- Put the mussels, finely chopped shallot, onion, herbs and white wine in a covered pot, bring to the boil and allow to simmer for 5 minutes.
- Take the mussels out of the shells, remove the beard and strain the liquid through a cloth.
- Sweat the julienne of vegetables in butter, add the fish stock and mussel stock and reduce.
- Add the cream.
- Put the mussels into the soup, remove from the heat and bind with the egg yolk and cream.
- Season the soup with salt and curry powder or freshly ground pepper.

▶

- Garnish with truffle in julienne strips and plucked chervil.

Note Mussels are very sandy and should, therefore be cleaned very carefully.

Soupe de poisson de mer
Fish soup with chervil

Ingredients (for 4 people)

1		sole, approximately 350g (12oz)
1		small sea bass, approximately 300g (11oz)
2		red mullet
4		scampi in shell
40cl	(¾ pint)	fish stock, well seasoned (see recipe 6)
20g	(¾oz)	leek ⎫
20g	(¾oz)	celery ⎬ cut into strips
20g	(¾oz)	carrot ⎭
30cl	(½ pint)	mussel stock, well strained (see recipe 8)
10cl	(4fl oz)	dry white wine (Muscadet)
8		mussels, freshly cooked and with beard removed
		salt, freshly ground pepper
		a little chervil
30g	(1¼oz)	diced tomato

Method
- Skin and fillet the sole and cut into thick strips.
- Descale and fillet the red mullet and sea bass and cut into thick strips.
- Break open the scampi.
- Use the fish bones and scampi shells for the fish stock (see recipe 6).

▶

- Cook the leek, celery and carrot until crisp in salty water and allow to cool in the same water on ice.
- Boil up the fish stock and mussel stock with the Muscadet in a suitable pan.
- Add the seasoned fish, scampi and mussels and allow to simmer for about 1-2 minutes (do not boil).
- Add the vegetables, season with salt and pepper.
- Just before serving add the chervil and diced tomatoes.

Note It is important that the pieces of fish are handled very carefully, otherwise they may easily fall apart. It is a good idea to use a skimming ladle to put the fish, mussels and scampi into the well seasoned soup. Freshly baked, crisp garlic bread goes very well with this soup.

Soupe de coquilles
St. Jacques Maître Camille
Scallop soup with julienne of vegetables

Camille Lurkan was the head chef at the world-famous restaurant, Villa Lorraine, in Brussels, where I had the pleasure of working for a short while.

Ingredients (for 4 people)

8		large scallops in their shells, (about 240g (8½oz) net)
20g	(¾oz)	carrot ⎫
30g	(1¼oz)	leek ⎬ cut into strips
30g	(1¼oz)	fennel ⎭
20g	(¾oz)	butter
20cl	(6fl oz)	mussel stock (see recipe 8)
20cl	(6fl oz)	fish stock (see recipe 6)
		salt, freshly ground pepper

▶

20cl	(6fl oz)	double cream
50g	(2oz)	butter, to finish
2cl	(¾fl oz)	Noilly Prat
4		slices of truffle

Method

- Open the scallops with a strong knife and place on the warm hotplate for a few minutes to open them completely.
- Remove the scallops and roe with a soup spoon. Carefully separate the scallops from the roe and wash thoroughly.
- Sweat the vegetables well in the butter, add the mussel stock and fish stock and allow to simmer for 2-3 minutes.
- Add the seasoned scallops and roe and simmer for 1 minute.
- Remove the scallops and vegetables and keep them hot in prepared soup bowls.
- Reduce the stock a little, add the cream, work in the soft butter, finish off with Noilly Prat and season to taste.
- Garnish with the truffles before serving.

Note It is important that the scallops are poached carefully to prevent them from drying out.

Chapter 5

Egg Dishes

Egg Dishes

On a menu the egg dishes are part of the small entrées. Generally one should reckon with two eggs per person. Eggs must always be eaten when absolutely fresh as much from a taste point of view as for nutritional and health reasons.

The usual chicken egg weighs on average 56g (2¼oz). At the same time, there are eggs weighing 35g (1¼oz) and also some weighing 80g (3oz). When using them in large quantities this variation can lead to weight differences, particularly in pastry recipes where exact weights are important. Most pastry chefs use the following table for working out the amount of liquid and weight for whole and split eggs:

     1 litre = 23-24 whole eggs
     1 litre = 35 egg whites
     1 litre = 44 egg yolks

An egg contains all the necessary nutritive substances for the creation of a living entity (water, protein, fat, mineral salts, vitamins A, B and C). The nutritional content of a whole egg is 6.5g (¼oz) protein and 5g (just under ¼oz) fat. Fresh eggs are light in colour and shine through evenly, older eggs appear somewhat cloudy. Eggs whose age is doubtful are lightly speckled and 'bad' eggs have dark patches on them.

Oeufs pochés au délice de saumon mariné

Poached eggs with marinated Scottish salmon

Ingredients (for 4 people)

12		thin slices of marinated salmon (see recipe 72)
4		eggs
8		lettuce hearts
		a little vinegar water
1cl	(½fl oz)	lemon juice
2cl	(¾fl oz)	walnut oil
		salt, freshly ground pepper
		a little dill for the garnish

Method

- Cut the salmon thinly as with smoked salmon.
- Poach the eggs carefully for about 5 minutes.
- Remove the poached eggs with a skimming ladle and cool in cold water.
- Place on a cloth and trim with a knife.
- Arrange the well washed and drained lettuce hearts attractively in a circle on a plate.
- Season with lemon juice, oil, salt and pepper.
- Place the eggs in the middle on the lettuce and garnish with the salmon and dill.
- Serve the sauce (see below) separately.

Sauce

15cl	(¼ pint)	sour cream
20g	(¾oz)	French mustard
3cl	(1¼fl oz)	liquid from the marinade, strained
		cayenne, salt, freshly ground pepper
		a little finely plucked dill

Method

- Mix everything together and season.

Samumon d'Écosse mariné
Marinated Scottish salmon

The idea for Saumon d'Écosse mariné comes from Scandinavia. I had the opportunity of working in the Grand Hotel in Stockholm where I got to know this recipe — a very good way to preserve fresh salmon without smoking it.

Ingredients (for 1.5kg salmon)

1.5kg	(3lb)	whole Scottish salmon
40g	(1½oz)	salt
25g	(1oz)	sugar
		plenty of dill
4cl	(1½fl oz)	oil
		peppercorns, coarsely ground

Method

- Carefully fillet the salmon and remove the bones.
- Cover with the mixture of condiments and dill, place in a suitable dish, cover and store in the refrigerator.
- Marinate the fish for 24 hours, occasionally moistening it with the liquid which is produced.
- Remove the dill and cut as smoked salmon.
- The dill may be used as garnish.

Oeufs de cailles aux poireaux
Quails' eggs with creamed leeks

Ingredients (for 4 people)

12		fresh quails' eggs
4		rectangular vol-au-vents of puff pastry, 8 × 4cm (3¼ × 1½in) (see recipe 19)
20cl	(6fl oz)	hollandaise sauce (see recipe 26)

Leek cream

100g	(4oz)	leeks, white and some green
10g	(½oz)	butter
5cl	(2fl oz)	poultry stock (see recipe 1)
5cl	(2fl oz)	Noilly Prat
5cl	(2fl oz)	double cream
		a little chopped tarragon
		salt, freshly ground pepper

Method

- Prick the quails' eggs several times with a pin.
- Place in boiling water and allow to simmer for 2½ minutes.
- Rinse the eggs immediately in cold water and then shell under running water.
- Make a small cut in the leeks so that they may be thoroughly washed and then cut into strips.
- Grease a suitable dish with butter, add the well dried leeks.
- Without adding any liquid, sweat slowly for about 8 minutes.
- Reduce the poultry stock and Noilly Prat to half their original volume.
- Add the double cream and reduce again until the required consistency is obtained.
- Add the liquid to the leeks.
- Put in the tarragon.
- Season with salt and pepper.
- Place the vol-au-vents on a piece of buttered greaseproof paper and, on a tray, bake until crisp in a pre-heated oven at about 250°C (480°F) for 15 to 18 minutes.
- Cut out the lids and keep warm.
- Arrange the vol-au-vents on a suitable dish while still warm.
- Fill with the well seasoned leek cream.
- Warm the quails' eggs in salted water and arrange on top.
- Carefully cover with hollandaise sauce.
- Garnish with the warm pastry lid and serve immediately. ▶

Note It is of particular importance that the eggs remain soft inside.

Oeufs mollets au ragoût fin
Soft boiled eggs with sweetbreads and mushrooms

This egg dish was on the à la carte menu in the world famous Beverly Wilshire Hotel in Los Angeles where we held a Dorchester speciality week in Spring 1978. It was much enjoyed by the guests.

Ingredients (for 4 people)

4		fresh eggs
150g	(5oz)	veal knuckle, boiled and cut into slices
60g	(2½oz)	sweetbreads, poached and plucked
60g	(2½oz)	steamed mushrooms, cut into cubes
20g	(¾oz)	butter
2g		finely chopped shallot
10cl	(4fl oz)	white wine
15cl	(¼ pint)	double cream
		salt, freshly ground pepper
10cl	(4fl oz)	hollandaise sauce (see recipe 26)
4		truffle slices

Method
- Boil the eggs for 5 minutes.
- Place in cold water to cool and then shell the eggs under running water.
- Sweat the sweetbreads, veal knuckle and mushrooms in the butter and shallot, add the white wine and reduce.
- Add the cream and reduce until the required consistency is achieved.
- Season with salt and pepper.

▶

- Arrange on a suitable dish and meanwhile warm the eggs in salt water. Arrange on top.
- Cover the eggs with hollandaise sauce and garnish with truffles.
- Serve immediately.

Oeufs en cocotte au caviar
Eggs in cocotte with caviar

Ingredients (for 4 people)

10g	(½oz)	butter
		salt, freshly ground pepper
4		eggs
10cl	(4fl oz)	double cream
40g	(1½oz)	caviar (Royal Beluga if possible)

Method
- Butter four individual cocotte dishes and season with salt and pepper.
- Put an egg in each one, cover and carefully poach in a bain-marie.
- Mix the slightly warmed cream with the caviar, season carefully and pour over the eggs.

Note It is important that the egg yolks remain slightly liquid. Only the egg white should be covered with the cream so that the yolks are still visible.

Oeufs brouillés aux cuisses de grenouilles
Scrambled eggs with frogs' legs

Ingredients (for 4 people)

10g	(½oz)	finely chopped shallots
20g	(¾oz)	butter
500g	(18oz)	small frogs' legs
		salt, freshly ground pepper
10cl	(4fl oz)	white wine (Alsace)
5cl	(2fl oz)	Noilly Prat
10cl	(4fl oz)	white veal stock (see recipe 2)
15cl	(¼ pint)	double cream
		a little thyme
		a little finely chopped parsley

Method

- Sweat the finely chopped shallots in butter.
- Add the seasoned frogs' legs and continue to sweat well (without browning them).
- Add the white wine, Noilly Prat and veal stock.
- Add the thyme, cover and allow to simmer for 5-6 minutes.
- Take the frogs' legs out of the stock and remove the meat from the bone.
- Reduce the stock a little.
- Add the cream and reduce to the required consistency.
- Put in the meat from the frogs' legs and season with salt, pepper and parsley.

Ingredients for the eggs

8		eggs
20g	(¾oz)	butter
3cl	(1¼fl oz)	double cream
		salt, a little freshly ground nutmeg
		freshly ground pepper

▶

Method

- Whisk the eggs well with a fork and strain through a fine sieve.
- Season with salt, nutmeg and pepper.
- Warm the butter in a sauteuse.
- Add the eggs and with a wooden spoon stir over a gentle heat until the mixture is bound.
- Mix in the cream just before the eggs are done.
- Season again.
- Arrange on a suitable dish, placing the frogs' legs ragoût in the middle of the scrambled eggs.
- Serve immediately.

Note It is important to wash the frogs' legs well before using them.

‘ All food should taste of what it is. ’

Chapter 6

Fish Dishes

Fish Dishes

There are countless different types of fish. With a few exceptions fish live in the wild. Depending on the water and also unfortunately upon the degree of pollution, they develop a special character both in their meat and in their taste. The gastronomer can therefore enjoy a wide choice.

Fish is wholesome because its meat is easily digestible. It has little connective tissue and is more easily digested than beef, but has the same nutritional value. What we are consuming when we eat meat, and of course fish, are cells and fibrous structures made up from different types of protein, water and fat. The water is contained partly inside the cell and partly in the proteins. In this state the water is bound and not able to run out. The denaturing process of protein is of enormous importance to the culinary quality of the dishes. At temperatures above 40°C (104°F) animal proteins start to coagulate, to congeal. (One is reminded of the protein in eggs.) At approximately 50°C (122°F) 40% to 50% of the protein has congealed and at 80°C (176°F) it is practically 100% fat. As a result the proteins change in structure and lose the ability to absorb and form water. The cells are no longer watertight and lose their cell liquid, i.e. the meat or fish juice runs out and both beefsteak and fish become hopelessly dry. Since the juice also carries the taste, juiceless meat also loses its flavour. If, when preparing fish, you make sure that the temperature never exceeds 55°C (131°F) you will never again serve dry fish.

The taste of fish
Generally, fish does not have an intensive taste but rather it has fine nuances of flavour which are nevertheless typical of many types of fish — pike, trout, salmon, etc. The water, of course, has something to do with this. It is now a maxim of good kitchens to retain the natural and

special taste of the food being prepared and only to help this along by the addition of suitable flavourings or to bring it out by contrasting it with certain garnishes and sauces.

Fresh fish have clear eyes and red gills. The flesh is firm to the touch and does not come away from the bone of its own accord. The scales lie firmly on the skin. The smell of the open gills should be fresh. Shortly before and shortly after the spawning season (close season) fish are generally less tasty and should not be served.

Fish protein is not protected by any binding agent. This means that the protein can easily be washed out by water. Therefore fish should never be steeped or left to soak in water, but should be stored on ice or covered with ice. Never leave filleted fish lying around, but instead remove the fillets just before using.

Fish is now one of the favourites of the modern kitchen. The main reason for this is that a good chef can do a great deal with and make a great deal out of fish, and can vary the methods of preparation and ingredients. In the preparation of fish the change in cooking practices can be seen most clearly; it is no longer overcooked but instead cooked, poached or baked for exactly the right length of time.

Mediterranean fish, such as loup de mer, rouget and turbot, are especially favoured in good kitchens and consequently by gourmets as well.

Turbot is called the pheasant of the sea because of its beauty.

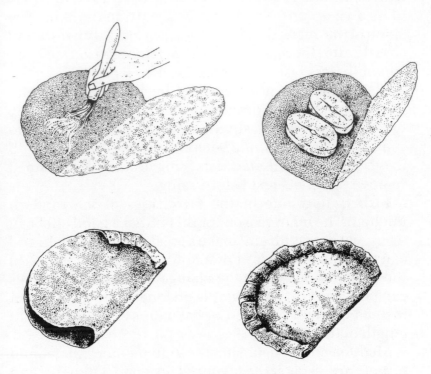

Four main stages in the preparation of Steak de saumon en papillote, fully described in the Method, opposite.

Steak de saumon en papillote
Salmon steak papillote-style

Ingredients (for 4 people)

750g	(1½lb)	salmon fillet, without the skin
		salt, freshly ground white pepper
50g	(2oz)	butter
40g	(1½oz)	onion, cut into thin strips
50g	(2oz)	carrots, cut into thin strips
60g	(2½oz)	leek, cut into thin strips
100g	(4oz)	mushrooms, raw and cut into thin strips
1cl	(½fl oz)	walnut oil
12		tarragon leaves
80g	(3oz)	butter
4cl	(1½fl oz)	dry white wine
4cl	(1½fl oz)	fish stock (see recipe 6)

Method

- Carefully remove the bones from the salmon and cut into four steaks.
- Season with salt and pepper.
- Heat 50g (2oz) butter in a suitable pan, add the onion and sweat.
- Add the carrots and leek and continue to sweat.
- Finally add the mushrooms and continue to sweat for a further 3 minutes.
- Add 4 tarragon leaves and season with salt and pepper.
- Prepare a piece of aluminium foil as in the illustrations opposite and about three times larger than the salmon steak and brush the inside with walnut oil.
- Distribute the vegetables on the foil.
- Arrange the seasoned salmon steak on top of the vegetables, put 20g (¾oz) of butter on each piece and garnish with tarragon leaves.

▶

- Add white wine and fish stock
- Carefully fold together the aluminium foil, making an airtight bag.
- Pack the aluminium foil in greaseproof paper, place on a baking tray and bake in a moderate oven for 15 to 18 minutes.

Note All en papillote dishes should be opened and served in front of the guest, because only then is the full taste and aroma brought out.

Escalope de truite saumonée aux poireaux
Salmon trout with leeks

Ingredients (for 4 people)

1		salmon trout (1 kg (2lb))
20g	(¾oz)	butter
		salt, freshly ground pepper
5cl	(2fl oz)	white wine (Chablis)
5cl	(2fl oz)	fish stock (see recipe 6)
1cl	(½fl oz)	melted butter, to pour over

Method
- Carefully fillet the salmon trout, removing the skin.
- Cut into four equal portions.
- Butter a suitable dish, put in the seasoned fish pieces, add the white wine and fish stock.
- Bring to the boil, cover and poach in the oven; the fish must remain pink.
- Remove the fish and keep warm.
- Reduce the stock to half its original volume, strain and reserve for the sauce.

▶

Sauce

25cl	(8fl oz)	fish stock (see recipe 6)
10cl	(4fl oz)	white wine
8cl	(3fl oz)	Noilly Prat
2g		finely chopped shallot
20cl	(6fl oz)	double cream
100g	(4oz)	butter, to finish
		salt, freshly ground pepper

Garnish

150g	(5oz)	young, tender leeks, well washed and cut into pieces 5cm (2in) long

Method

- Reduce the fish stock, white wine, Noilly Prat and shallot.
- Add the cream and reduce to the required consistency.
- Strain and add the fish stock which has been used to poach the salmon trout.
- Carefully monté with the soft butter.
- Blanch the leeks for a short time and add to the sauce.
- Season with salt and pepper.
- Arrange on a suitable dish and place the pieces of salmon trout on top.
- Sprinkle the fish with the melted butter and serve immediately.

Escalope de truite saumonée aux poireaux

Salmon trout with leeks

Second version

Ingredients (for 4 people)

1		salmon trout (1 kg (2lb))
20g	(¾oz)	butter, for greasing the baking tray
		salt, freshly ground white pepper
		sauce (see recipe 78)
1cl	(½fl oz)	melted butter, to pour over

Method
- Fillet the salmon trout carefully, removing the skin.
- Cut the fish into pieces approximately 1.5cm (½in) thick and 6 to 7cm (2¼in) long.
- Season the fish pieces, lay them on the buttered baking tray and cook them for 2 to 3 minutes on each side, either in the oven with a strong heat coming from the top or under the grill. The fish must remain pink.
- Make the hot sauce (see recipe 78), place the fish on top, pour on the melted butter and serve immediately.

Saumon d'Écosse Maître Schlegel

Salmon soufflé with pike mousseline

This dish was one of the specialities of the Palace Hotel in Lucerne. The dish was invented in honour of Otto Schlegel who was head chef in this hotel for 26 years. Otto Schlegel also spent 26 seasons in the world-famous Palace Hotel, Gstaad. I had the pleasure of working for four very enjoyable and instructive seasons with Mr Schlegel, a superb master of his profession.

Ingredients (for 4 people)

1kg	(2lb)	salmon (about 480g (18oz))
		salt, freshly ground pepper
2g		finely chopped shallot
150g	(5oz)	mousseline of pike (see recipe 14)
4		scampi without their shells
20g	(¾oz)	butter
10cl	(4fl oz)	white wine
10cl	(4fl oz)	fish stock (see recipe 6)
5cl	(2fl oz)	Noilly Prat
40cl	(¾ pint)	double cream
50g	(2oz)	butter, to finish
		a little sorrel, cut into strips
5cl	(2fl oz)	lobster sauce (see recipe 23)

Method

- Fillet the salmon carefully, removing all skin and bones and cutting it into 4 portions.
- Cover the seasoned salmon portions evenly with the pike mousseline.
- Lay the seasoned scampi on top, pressing them gently into the mousseline. ▶

- Grease a sautoir and sprinkle with the finely chopped shallot.
- Arrange the salmon portions in it.
- Add the white wine and fish stock, cover and poach in the oven.
- Remove the fish and keep hot.
- Add the Noilly Prat. Reduce the stock, add the cream and reduce until the required consistency is achieved.
- Gradually work in the butter, add sorrel and season with salt and pepper.
- Place the salmon briefly under the grill or in a hot oven to give it a good colour.
- Place the sauce in a suitable dish and arrange the salmon on it.
- Carefully cover the scampi with the well seasoned lobster sauce.

Filets des danseuses de rivière à la ciboulette

Fresh river trout fillets with chives

Ingredients (for 4 people)

6		freshly killed rainbow trout (180g (6oz) each)
10g	(½oz)	butter
5g	(¼oz)	celery, cut into slices
5g	(¼oz)	leek, cut into small pieces
		salt, freshly ground white pepper
15cl	(¼ pint)	dry white wine (Dézaley)
		a little cornflour
150g	(5oz)	butter, to finish
		a few chives, finely chopped
		a little cayenne

▶

Method

- Cut the trout and fillet them carefully with a sharp knife.
- Grease a suitable dish with butter and place the celery and leek in it.
- Put in the seasoned trout fillets, add the white wine, cover with butter paper and poach.
- Take out the trout fillets, remove the skin and keep warm.
- Reduce the stock almost to a glaze.
- Bind the stock with cornflour.
- Remove the pan from the heat and gradually work in the soft butter, if necessary adding a little white wine.
- Add the finely chopped chives to the sauce and season with salt, white pepper and cayenne.
- Arrange the trout fillets on a plate and cover with the very light sauce.
- Serve immediately.

Note When working in the butter at the end, it is important that the pan is neither too hot nor too cold, otherwise the sauce will curdle.

Suprême de sole Philippe

Fillets of sole with
white wine sauce and prawns

Ingredients (for 4 people)

2		sole (approximately 400g (14oz))
10g	(½oz)	butter
2g		finely chopped shallot
		salt, freshly ground white pepper
10cl	(4fl oz)	dry white wine
10cl	(4fl oz)	fish stock (see recipe 6)
40cl	(¾ pint)	double cream
2cl	(¾fl oz)	Armagnac
80g	(3¼oz)	butter, to finish
12		prawns with their heads
60g	(2½oz)	mushrooms, cut into thick strips and poached
4		puff pastry fleurons, cut into shape of a starfish (see recipe 19)

Method

- Remove the skin from both sides of the sole and fillet.
- Grease a suitable dish with butter and sprinkle with shallot.
- Season and fold over the fillets of sole and place side by side in the dish.
- Add the white wine and fish stock, cover with butter paper and poach in the oven.
- Remove the fillets of sole and keep warm, reduce the stock.
- Add the cream and reduce until the required consistency is achieved.
- Finish off with the Armagnac, monté with butter and season with salt and pepper.
- Arrange the fillets of sole and cover with the sauce.
- Warm the prawns in the stock and use as a garnish with the poached mushrooms and freshly baked fleurons.

Timbale de sole Eugène Käufeler

Sole and lobster timbale Eugène Käufeler

Mr Käufeler worked at the Dorchester for 42 years and for 26 of those was *Maître-Chef des Cuisines*. He offered me the position as his successor in the Dorchester. A chef of world-wide reputation, he created this recipe, which commemorates his achievements.

Ingredients (for 4 people)

480g	(18oz)	filleted sole, cut into thick strips
		salt, freshly ground pepper
10g	(½oz)	lobster butter (see recipe 35)
10g	(½oz)	finely chopped shallot
60g	(2½oz)	mushrooms, sliced
80g	(3oz)	lobster flesh
10cl	(4fl oz)	Sherry
10cl	(4fl oz)	white wine
20cl	(6fl oz)	lobster sauce (see recipe 23)
20cl	(6fl oz)	double cream
4		halves of lobster claws } to garnish
4		pieces of truffle, sliced }

Method

- Season the pieces of sole.
- Sweat the shallot in the lobster butter.
- Add the seasoned pieces of sole and sauté for one minute.
- Add the mushrooms and lobster meat.
- Add the Sherry and white wine.
- Remove the pieces of sole, mushrooms and lobster and keep warm. Reduce the stock.
- Add the lobster sauce and cream and reduce until the required consistency is obtained.

▶

- Fill the pieces of sole, mushrooms and lobster into timbales and cover with the seasoned sauce.
- Use the warm lobster claws and truffle slices as garnish.

Note Pilaf rice makes a particularly good accompaniment to this dish.

Paupiettes de sole Montrose
*Paupiettes of sole with
smoked salmon*

Ingredients (for 4 people)

2		sole (about 350g (12oz) each)
		salt, freshly ground white pepper
8		pieces of smoked salmon, finely cut
20g	(¾oz)	butter
2g		finely chopped shallot
20g	(¾oz)	carrot ⎫
20g	(¾oz)	leek ⎬ cut into strips
20g	(¾oz)	celery ⎭
20cl	(6fl oz)	white wine
5cl	(1½fl oz)	Noilly Prat
10cl	(4fl oz)	fish stock (see recipe 6)
30cl	(½ pint)	double cream
10cl	(4fl oz)	lobster sauce (see recipe 23)

Method

- Remove the skin from both sides of the sole and then fillet them.
- Flatten the fillets of sole lightly, season and lay the slices of smoked salmon on them.
- Roll them up and hold together with a cocktail stick.
- Grease a suitable dish with butter, sprinkle with the shallot and add the carrot, leek and celery.
- Add the paupiettes of sole, white wine, Noilly Prat and fish stock, cover and poach in the oven.

▶

- Remove the paupiettes and vegetables and keep warm.
- Reduce the stock, add the cream and lobster sauce and reduce to the required consistency.
- Add the strips of vegetables to the sauce and season to taste with salt and pepper.
- Cover the paupiettes with the light sauce.

Goujons de sole aux oranges et poivre vert
Goujons of sole with oranges and green peppercorns

Ingredients (for 4 people)

8		fillets of sole, cut into strips approximately 10g (½oz) each salt, freshly ground pepper a little orange peel, finely chopped
10g	(½oz)	butter
5cl	(2fl oz)	fish stock (see recipe 6)
4cl	(1½fl oz)	white wine, rather sweet
5cl	(2fl oz)	Noilly Prat
20		green peppercorns
60g	(2½oz)	turnips, turned to the size of a garlic clove and blanched
40g	(1½oz)	butter, to finish
2		oranges, cut into segments
8		small basil leaves

Method
- Marinate the fillets of sole with salt, pepper and a little orange peel.
- Grease a sauteuse with butter, put in the pieces of sole, fish stock, white wine and Noilly Prat, cover and poach for about 1½ minutes on each side until glassy.

▶

- Remove the fish and keep warm, reduce the stock to the required consistency.
- Add the green peppercorns and the blanched turnips.
- Very gradually work in the butter and season with salt and pepper.
- Return the pieces of sole to the sauce, add the orange slices. Arrange in a dish, garnish with the basil leaves and serve immediately.

Suprême de turbot à la moëlle
Turbot fillets with marrow

Ingredients (for 4 people)

4		pieces turbot fillet (150g (5oz) each)
		salt, freshly ground pepper
3cl	(1¼fl oz)	peanut oil
80g	(3¼oz)	butter
160g	(5½oz)	beef marrow, diced
30g	(1¼oz)	white breadcrumbs
		a little chopped parsley
3cl	(1¼fl oz)	white wine
4		lemon halves to garnish

Method
- Sauté the seasoned turbot in the oil and some of the butter.
- Mix together the marrow, breadcrumbs, parsley and white wine, and season with salt and pepper.
- Spread this mixture evenly on the turbot fillets and glaze under the grill.
- Arrange in a suitable dish.
- Top with the rest of the butter, heated until brown and foaming.
- Garnish with lemon and serve immediately.

Tronçon de turbot soufflé aux écrevisses
Turbot soufflé with crayfish

Ingredients (for 4 people)

4		turbot tronçons (130g (4¾oz) each)
160g	(5½oz)	pike mousseline (see recipe 14)
5g	(¼oz)	butter
2g		finely chopped shallot
		salt, freshly ground pepper
10cl	(4fl oz)	Noilly Prat
30cl	(½ pint)	fish stock (see recipe 6)
30cl	(½ pint)	single cream
40g	(1½oz)	butter, to finish
4		chervil sprigs
100g	(4oz)	cucumber, turned and blanched
4		freshwater crayfish, with tails removed but not discarded
4		slices of truffle
4		puff pastry fleurons (see recipe 19)

Method (See Plate 11)

- Remove the bones from the turbot tronçons.
- Stuff with the pike mousseline.
- Line a suitable sautoir with butter and the finely chopped shallot, arrange the four tronçons on top, season, add the Noilly Prat and the fish stock, cover and poach in the oven.
- Remove the fish, reduce the stock, add the cream and reduce to the required consistency. Gradually work in the butter.
- Add the chervil sprigs, season with salt and pepper.
- Remove the skin from the tronçons, arrange in a suitable dish and cover with the well seasoned sauce.

▶

- Garnish with the turned cucumber, the crayfish tails, which have been warmed in the stock, and the truffle slices.
- Use the bodies of the crayfish and the fleurons to garnish.

Note Pieces of scallops, lobster, truffles or prawns may also be added to the pike mousseline.

Blanc de turbot parfumé à la moutarde
Turbot fillets with mustard sauce

Ingredients (for 4 people)

4		turbot fillets (160g (5½oz) each)
		salt, freshly ground pepper
20g	(¾oz)	butter
20cl	(6fl oz)	white wine
10cl	(4fl oz)	fish stock (see recipe 6)
2g		finely chopped shallot
20cl	(6fl oz)	double cream
60g	(2½oz)	butter, to finish
5g	(¼oz)	Dijon mustard
30g	(1¼oz)	whipped cream
		a little lemon juice
4		puff pastry fleurons (see recipe 19)

Method
- Fillet and season the turbot, place in a buttered sauteuse with the chopped shallot so that they are ready for poaching.
- Add the white wine and fish stock, cover and poach in the oven.
- Remove the fillets and keep warm.

▶

- Reduce the fish stock, add the double cream and reduce until the required consistency is achieved.
- Gradually work in the butter and mustard.
- Carefully mix in the whipped cream, season with salt, pepper and a little lemon juice.
- Arrange the fish on a plate, cover with the sauce and brown under the grill.
- Garnish with the fleurons.

Goujons de turbot au safran
Goujons of turbot with saffron

Ingredients (for 4 people)

700g	(1½lb)	turbot fillets
5g	(¼oz)	butter
2g		finely chopped shallot
25		shreds of saffron
5cl	(2fl oz)	dry white wine
4cl	(1½fl oz)	Noilly Prat
8cl	(3fl oz)	fish stock (see recipe 6)
		salt, freshly ground pepper
15cl	(¼ pint)	double cream
30g	(1¼oz)	diced tomato
100g	(4oz)	cucumber, cut out with a Parisienne spoon and blanched
		a few tarragon leaves without stalks
50g	(2oz)	unsalted butter, to finish
		a few drops of Pernod

Method
- Cut the turbot fillets into strips, 15g (½oz) each.
- Melt the butter in a suitable pan and put in the shallot and saffron.
- Sweat well and add the white wine, Noilly Prat and fish stock.

►

- Put in the seasoned pieces of turbot and simmer for about 5 minutes (do not boil).
- Remove the fish and keep warm.
- Reduce the stock, add the cream and reduce to the required consistency.
- Add the diced tomato and blanched cucumber to the sauce.
- Season with tarragon leaves.
- Monté the sauce with butter, flavour with a little Pernod, salt and pepper.
- Mix the sauce with the turbot fillets and serve immediately.

Filet de turbot aux huîtres
Fillet of turbot with oysters and julienne of vegetables

Ingredients (for 4 people)

15g	(½oz)	butter
5g	(¼oz)	finely chopped shallot
4		turbot fillets (180g (6oz) each)
		salt, freshly ground pepper
10cl	(4fl oz)	Champagne
		juice of ¼ lemon
16		oysters
20g	(¾oz)	carrot
20g	(¾oz)	celery } cut into fine strips
20g	(¾oz)	leek
60g	(2½oz)	butter, to finish

Method
- Butter a suitable dish, sprinkle with the chopped shallot and place the seasoned fish on top.
- Add the Champagne and lemon juice, cover and poach carefully in the oven.

▶

- Remove the turbot fillets and keep warm. Strain the stock.
- Open the oysters, remove the beard, strain the oyster water through a fine sieve or muslin.
- Lay the oysters in their own water until needed.
- Sweat the carrot, celery and leek in butter without giving them any colour.
- Add the stock to the vegetables and the oysters and their water.
- Poach the oysters in the stock for about 15 seconds without boiling and keep warm.
- Reduce the stock to half its original volume and remove from the heat.
- Carefully monté with butter.
- Season the sauce with salt and pepper, arrange on a plate with the fish on top and the oysters as garnish.
- Serve immediately.

Epigramme de flétan 'Maître Jules'
Fillet of halibut with seafood and grapes

Ingredients (for 4 people)

4		halibut fillets (150g (5oz) each)
		salt, freshly ground pepper
10cl	(4fl oz)	oil
4		scallops, sliced
2		sole fillets, cut into strips of 60g
4		scampi, with shells removed (2½oz)
50g	(2oz)	butter
4		river crayfish with shells removed
20	(¾oz)	white Muscatel grapes, peeled and stoned
20g	(¾oz)	walnuts, peeled and cut in half
		a little parsley, chopped

►

Method

- Sauté the seasoned halibut fillets in oil until golden brown.
- Season the scallops, fillets of sole and scampi and sauté in brown butter, add the crayfish tails, grapes and walnuts.
- Arrange everything on top of the halibut fillets and sprinkle with brown butter.
- Use the four crayfish as garnish and decorate with chopped parsley.

Note The special quality of this dish is well displayed in the combination of fish, walnuts and grapes.

Filet de flétan en laitue
Fillet of halibut in lettuce leaves

Ingredients (for 4 people)

4		pieces of halibut fillet (160g (5½oz) each) salt, freshly ground pepper
8		blanched lettuce leaves
2g		finely chopped shallot
20g	(¾oz)	butter
40g	(1½oz)	leeks ⎫
40g	(1½oz)	carrot ⎬ cut into julienne strips
40g	(1½oz)	celery ⎭
15cl	(¼ pint)	white wine
30cl	(½ pint)	fish stock (see recipe 6)
30cl	(½ pint)	double cream
80g	(3¼oz)	butter, to finish

Method

- Roll the seasoned halibut in the lettuce leaves.

▶

- Grease a suitable dish, place the shallot and halibut in the dish, arrange a julienne of vegetables on top, add white wine and fish stock, cover, bring to the boil quickly and then poach in the oven.
- Remove the fish and julienne and keep warm.
- Reduce the stock, add the cream and reduce until the required consistency is achieved.
- Monté with the soft butter and season with salt and pepper.
- Cover the fish and vegetables with the sauce.

Note When blanched the lettuce leaves become slightly bitter which gives a pleasant taste to this dish. It is important that the vegetables remain slightly crisp.

Suprême d'aigrefin Élysée
Haddock fillets with green asparagus

Ingredients (for 4 people)

4		smoked haddock fillets, (160g (5½oz) each)
2g		finely chopped shallot
10cl	(4fl oz)	dry white wine
20cl	(6fl oz)	fish stock (see recipe 6)
20g	(¾oz)	butter
40cl	(¾ pint)	double cream
100g	(4oz)	tomatoes, diced
		a little chopped parsley
60g	(2½oz)	butter, to finish
		salt, freshly ground pepper
12		green asparagus tips, blanched

Method
- Poach the carefully trimmed haddock fillets with the shallot, white wine and fish stock in a buttered dish.
- Remove the haddock fillets and reduce the stock.

▶

- Add the cream and reduce to the required consistency.
- Add the tomatoes and chopped parsley and monté with butter.
- Season with salt and pepper and cover the fillets with the sauce.
- Warm the asparagus tips in butter and use as garnish.

Grenadins de baudroie à la sauce verte
Monkfish with green sauce

Ingredients (for 4 people)

1		monkfish weighing 1.5kg (3lb)
10g	(½oz)	butter
2g		finely chopped shallot
		salt, freshly ground pepper
20cl	(6fl oz)	dry white wine
20cl	(6fl oz)	fish stock (see recipe 6)
80g	(3oz)	butter, to finish
20g	(¾oz)	purée of chives with juice

Method
- Carefully pull off the skin of the monkfish and remove any dark patches.
- Remove the flesh from the gristle in the middle of the fish.
- Cut the well trimmed fillets into 16 pieces weighing approximately 40g (1½oz) each.
- Grease a suitable dish with butter and sprinkle with the shallot.
- Season the pieces of fish with salt and pepper and add to the dish.
- Add the white wine and fish stock.
- Cover with butter paper and poach in the oven for 8-10 minutes.

- Remove the pieces of fish from the stock and keep warm.
- Reduce the stock to half its original volume and carefully monté with the butter which should not be too soft.
- Add the purée of chives and juice.
- Strain through a fine sieve and season with salt and pepper.
- Pour the sauce on to a warm dish.
- Arrange the fish on the sauce and serve immediately.

Note There are various English names for baudroie (or lotte) — monkfish is the most common, but angler fish is frequently used.

Queue de lotte grillée aux herbes
Grilled monkfish tail with fresh herbs

Anyone who has travelled in Provence and has experienced the smell of the aromatic herbs, is well able to imagine this dish — simple, natural and tasty.

Ingredients (for 4 people)

4		monk fish tails (200g (7oz)) without bones
10cl	(4fl oz)	olive oil
8g	(½oz)	herb mixture (dill, basil, thyme and marjoram) garlic
		salt, freshly ground pepper
		a little parsley to garnish
15cl	(¼ pint)	melted butter

Method
- Carefully remove the skin from the fish and trim well.
- Marinate the pieces of fish in olive oil, the herb mixture and garlic for about an hour. ▶

- Remove the pieces of fish from the marinade, season with salt and pepper and grill on both sides.
- Arrange on a suitable dish and garnish with the parsley.
- Serve the melted butter separately.

Note Be careful not to let the herb mixture burn during grilling. Boiled new potatoes go well with this dish.

Queue de lotte au poivre noir
Monkfish tail with black peppercorns

Ingredients (for 4 people)

800g	(1¾lb)	monkfish tail cut into slices
		a few crushed black peppercorns
20g	(¾oz)	butter
5g	(¼oz)	finely chopped shallot
20cl	(6fl oz)	white wine
30cl	(½ pint)	double cream
15g	(½oz)	fish glaze (see recipe 9)
10g	(½oz)	butter
		salt, cayenne
20g	(¾oz)	small fresh morels
4		puff pastry fleurons (see recipe 19)

Method
- Season the pieces of fish with the crushed peppercorns and salt and sweat them in the butter and shallot without browning them.
- Add the white wine and reduce.
- Add the cream and fish glaze, cover and simmer for 6-7 minutes.
- Remove the fish and keep warm.
- Reduce the sauce to the required consistency.
- Season well with salt and cayenne.

▶

- Arrange the fish with the sauce.
- Garnish with morels sautéd in butter and freshly-baked fleurons.

Filets de St. Pierre sans nom
Fillets of John Dory in white wine sauce with tomatoes

Ingredients (for 4 people)

2		John Dory fish weighing about 1.5kg (3lb)
30g	(1¼oz)	butter
		salt, freshly ground white pepper
5cl	(2fl oz)	dry white wine
5cl	(2fl oz)	fish stock (see recipe 6)
		a little lemon juice
160g	(5½oz)	tomates concassés (see recipe 36)

Method
- Wash the John Dory thoroughly and, using a filleting knife, carefully remove the fillets.
- Remove the skin from the fillets and trim.
- Grease a suitable dish with butter.
- Season the fish with salt and pepper and place in the dish.
- Add the white wine and fish stock and sprinkle with lemon juice.
- Cover with a butter paper, bring to the boil and poach in the oven for 3 or 4 minutes, until just done.
- Remove the fillets and keep warm.
- Reduce the stock a little, strain and add to the sauce, (see below).
- Arrange the hot and well seasoned tomatoes concassés on a plate.
- Place the John Dory fillets on top and cover with the well-seasoned sauce.
- Serve immediately. ▶

Recipes 96 & 97

Sauce

6cl	(2½fl oz)	Noilly Prat
6cl	(2½fl oz)	dry white wine
5cl	(2fl oz)	fish stock (see recipe 6)
2		egg yolks
		a little lemon juice
2g		finely cut chives
		salt, freshly ground white pepper, cayenne

Method

- Reduce the Noilly Prat, dry white wine and fish stock to half their original volume.
- Allow to cool a little.
- Add the egg yolks, put in a bain-marie and beat until stiff like a sabayon.
- Flavour with lemon juice.
- Add the finely cut chives and season with salt, pepper and cayenne.

‘ Great men have said that more marriages are ruined by bad cooking than through any other cause. The young wife's efforts at cooking have become one of the comedian's stock jokes. But the world has done little to fight this destructive cause of marital unhappiness. Good food, well cooked, goes hand in hand with married bliss. ’

Biscuit de barbue à la crème d'oursins
Mousse of brill with sea-urchin sauce

Ingredients (for 4 people)

750g	(26oz)	brill
		salt, freshly ground pepper
40cl	(¾ pint)	double cream
10g	(½oz)	butter, for lining the moulds

Method
- Fillet the brill and pass through a fine sieve.
- Place in a bowl on ice, season with salt and pepper.
- Vigorously work in the cream, little by little.
- Push the mixture again through a hair sieve and keep cool.
- Grease small soufflé moulds with butter and add the mixture.
- Poach in a bain-marie in a pre-heated oven for about 15 minutes.
- Allow the mousse to rest for a little while in the moulds before serving.
- Arrange for serving and cover with the following delicately seasoned sauce.

Sauce

6		sea-urchins
20cl	(6fl oz)	fish stock (see recipe 6)
30cl	(½ pint)	double cream
		salt, freshly ground pepper

Method
- Cut out the sea-urchins on the flat side with kitchen scissors, spoon out the tongues, and put to one side in a bowl.

▶

- Reduce the fish stock, add the cream and reduce to the required consistency then add the sea-urchin tongue with the liquid.
- Season with salt and pepper.

Note In order to obtain uniformly shaped biscuits, it is a good idea to tap the moulds, when filling them with the mousse, so that the air can escape.

Filets de rouget à la vapeur sous cloche
Fillets of red mullet with vinaigrette sauce

Ingredients (for 4 people)

8		whole red mullet (approximately 160g (5½oz) each) salt, freshly ground pepper
20g	(¾oz)	carrot, cannelé and sliced
20g	(¾oz)	small onions, finely chopped
8		small basil leaves

Method (See Plate 10)
- Gut the red mullet, wash thoroughly and carefully fillet them.
- Cut out some notches on the skin side of the fish with a sharp knife (three incisions per fillet).
- Steam the seasoned fillets for about 3-4 minutes.
- Arrange under a cloche with the skin turned upwards.
- Cover with the finely seasoned sauce vinaigrette (see below).
- Garnish with the well blanched carrots and onions and the basil leaves.

▶

PLATE 9
Above: Mousseline de coquilles St.Jacques. Mousseline of scallops with fresh tomato purée. *(Recipe 57).*

Left: Elixir de cailles aux oeufs. Clear quail soup with soft egg. *(Recipe 61).*

PLATE 10 *(Overleaf)*
Filet de rouget à la vapeur sous cloche. Fillets of red mullet with vinaigrette sauce *(Recipe 99).*

Sauce vinaigrette

5cl	(2fl oz)	red wine vinegar
10cl	(4fl oz)	olive oil
5g	(¼oz)	finely chopped shallot
		a little parsley and basil
		salt, freshly ground pepper

Method

- Mix together thoroughly the vinegar, oil and chopped shallot.
- Add the parsley and basil and season with salt and pepper.

Note This dish can also be served as a first course. In this case, use only half the ingredient quantities.

Filets des perches aux petites légumes
Fillets of perch with vegetables and chives

Ingredients (for 4 people)

1.8kg	(3½lb)	whole perch (approximately 800g (26oz) fillets)
20g	(¾oz)	butter
4g	(¼oz)	finely chopped shallot
20g	(¾oz)	carrot ⎫
20g	(¾oz)	leek ⎬ cut into strips
20g	(¾oz)	celery ⎭
20cl	(6fl oz)	dry white wine
20cl	(6fl oz)	fish stock (see recipe 6)
30cl	(½ pint)	double cream
50g	(2oz)	butter, to finish
		finely chopped chives
		salt, freshly ground pepper

▶

Method
- Skin the perch, fillet and wash them carefully.
- Grease a suitable dish and put in the shallot and vegetables.
- Arrange the seasoned perch fillets on top.
- Add white wine and fish stock, cover with butter paper, bring quickly to the boil and poach in the oven for 3-4 minutes.
- Remove the fillets and keep warm.
- Reduce the stock, add the cream and reduce until the required consistency is achieved.
- Gradually work in the butter, add the chives and season with salt and pepper.
- Cover the fillets with the sauce.

Note Pommes à la vapeur is the best garniture to serve with this delicate dish.

Quenelles de brochet 'Mère Olga'

Poached pike quenelles 'Mère Olga'

Ingredients (for 4 people)

250g	(9oz)	pike flesh without skin
		salt, freshly ground white pepper
1		egg white
25cl	(8fl oz)	double cream
1 litre	(1¾ pints)	fish stock (see recipe 6)
200g	(7oz)	blanched spinach
40g	(1½oz)	butter
5g	(¼oz)	finely chopped shallot
100g	(4oz)	mushrooms, cut into slices
20cl	(6fl oz)	crayfish sauce (see recipe 24)
20cl	(6fl oz)	white wine sauce (see below)
4		halves of crayfish tail

▶

8		thin slices of truffle
4		puff pastry fleurons (see recipe 19)
		filled with caviar

Method
- Mince the pike flesh well and place in a bowl on ice.
- Season and stir in the egg white.
- Gradually mix in the cream, stirring all the time.
- Season the mousse and push through a sieve.
- With the help of two spoons form 8 equally-sized quenelles and carefully poach them in the well seasoned fish stock.
- Sweat the spinach in the butter with chopped shallot and mushrooms.
- Arrange the quenelles on the spinach and cover half of them with crayfish sauce and the other half with white wine sauce (see below).
- Garnish with the crayfish tails, heated truffle slices and fleurons.

Note Cut the warm fleurons in half, fill with caviar, replace the lid at an angle and serve immediately.

White wine sauce
10g	(½oz)	finely chopped shallot
5g	(¼oz)	butter
10cl	(4fl oz)	Chablis
20cl	(7fl oz)	fish stock (see recipe 6)
2cl	(¾fl oz)	Noilly Prat
10cl	(4fl oz)	double cream
40g	(1½oz)	butter, to finish
		salt, freshly ground pepper

Method
- Sweat the shallot in the butter.
- Add the wine, fish stock and Noilly Prat and reduce almost completely.
- Strain through a fine sieve.
- Add the cream and put in the liquidiser.
- Cut the butter into cubes, add and liquidise.
- Season with salt and pepper.

Timbale de brochet Palace
Timbale of pike with spinach and lobster

Ingredients (for 4 people)

600g	(1¼lbs)	mousseline of pike (see recipe 14)
80g	(3¼oz)	cooked and well strained spinach
10g	(½oz)	raw lobster coral
		salt, freshly ground white pepper and a little cayenne
4		turned mushroom caps
5g	(¼oz)	butter

Method

- Divide the mousseline between three dishes.
- Mix the spinach and lobster coral equally into two dishes of mousseline and season with salt, pepper and cayenne.
- Grease the timbale moulds.
- Fill with pike, spinach and lobster mousse.
- Poach carefully in a bain-marie in the oven for about 15 minutes.
- Remove from the moulds and arrange on a plate which has the sauce (see below) on it.
- Warm the mushrooms in butter and use as garnish on top.

Note It is advisable to leave the timbale moulds to rest for about 5 minutes after poaching so that the mousse comes away more easily.

Sauce

10cl	(4fl oz)	white wine
5cl	(2fl oz)	vermouth
40cl	(¾ pint)	double cream
		some basil leaves
		salt and freshly ground white pepper

▶

Method
- Reduce the white wine and vermouth, add the cream and again reduce. Season with chopped basil leaves, salt and pepper.

Anguilles vertes
Eels in herb sauce

Ingredients (for 4 people)

1kg	(2lb)	fresh eels
100g	(4oz)	spinach, finely chopped
50g	(2oz)	sorrel, sweated in butter
30g	(1¼oz)	watercress, sweated in butter
2g		tarragon
5g	(¼oz)	chervil, finely chopped
5g	(¼oz)	parsley, finely chopped
2cl	(¾fl oz)	olive oil
		salt, freshly ground pepper

Method
- Skin the eels and cut into pieces 5-6cm (2-2¼in) long.
- Liquidise the vegetables and herbs.
- Add the herb infusion (see below) and reduce to a third of its original volume.
- Season the eel flesh and sauté in oil until golden brown. Remove the eel from the fat and place in the liquid.
- Cover and cook for about 10 minutes.
- Season with salt and pepper and serve in a suitable dish.

Herb infusion

10g	(½oz)	nettles
10g	(½oz)	pimpernel
5g	(¼oz)	grated ginger

►

Recipes 102 & 103

Method

- Pour some boiling water over the nettles, pimpernel and ginger and leave to infuse for 20 minutes.
- Strain through a muslin sieve.

Chapter 7

Shellfish Dishes

Shellfish Dishes

Scallops After leaving the water scallops live for about 30-36 hours. I would recommend buying only closed scallops. After opening them, tap the edge of the shell so that the flesh comes away easily. This freshness test is infallible. The same thing can be achieved with salt—the scallop should move immediately.

Lobster Female lobsters from Brittany or the Irish and Scottish coasts guarantee the best taste. They are bluish white in colour or light blue with white marks. The meat of the female tastes better because the males run too much, do not feed properly and exhaust themselves with their love affairs! Because of their claws, they work more than is to be recommended for the development of a pleasant taste. Apart from this, the head of the female contains a very delicate strip of meat, whereas the head of the male does not. Pregnant females have the best lobster taste. One can tell the sex of a lobster by comparing the width of the shell underneath; the female shell is bigger in order to hold her eggs. The ideal weight is 800-900g (1¾-2lb).

Oysters The biggest oysters are by no means the best. The best ones are considered to be the real Belon oysters which come from the river of the same name. They are pleasantly fat, somewhat salty and have a slightly nutty taste. If possible, oysters should be opened 15 minutes before eating.

Crayfish The best crayfish are the ones with red legs. These river crayfish are darker and have meatier and shorter claws than those with white legs which come from stagnant water. Apart from this, those with red legs have firmer, finer and tastier meat than those with white legs. Most red-legged river crayfish today come from Poland.

‘ The most interesting guests for any cook are those who do not have standardised tastes. ’

Rendez-vous de fruits-de-mer à la crème de basilic

Seafood in basil sauce

Why the name rendez-vous? One of my principles is to retain flexibility in cooking. A rendez-vous allows a lot of scope — one is not obliged to serve coquilles St. Jacques, lobster or sole but rather whatever comes completely fresh from the market so that the best produce of the day can be offered to the guest. Personally, I think the name 'rendez-vous' makes the guest curious and he orders the dish just to have a surprise.

Ingredients (for 4 people)

4		large scallops in their shells 120g (4½oz) net
8		scampi, removed from their shells
140g	(5oz)	salmon, cut into pieces lengthwise 15g (½oz)
140g	(5oz)	turbot, cut into pieces lengthwise 15g (½oz)
4		oysters, in their shells
20g	(¾oz)	carrot
20g	(¾oz)	leek } cut into thin strips
20g	(¾oz)	celery
20g	(¾oz)	butter
20cl	(6fl oz)	fish stock (see recipe 6)
20cl	(6fl oz)	dry white wine
40cl	(¾ pint)	double cream
4cl	(1½fl oz)	Noilly Prat
12		basil leaves, cut into strips
60g	(2½oz)	butter, to finish salt, freshly ground pepper cayenne

Method (See Plate 7)

- Open the scallops with a small strong knife and place on the hotplate for a few minutes to open them completely. Remove the scallops and roe with a soup

▶

Recipe 104

spoon. Separate the scallops carefully from the roe and wash thoroughly.
- Cut the scallops in half and lay on a cloth to dry.
- Season the scampi and pieces of salmon and turbot.
- Open the oysters, take out the flesh and remove the beards (keep the oysters in their own water).
- Sweat the carrot, leek and celery in the butter.
- Add the turbot and scampi and continue to sweat.
- Add the salmon and scallops.
- Add the fish stock and white wine, bring to the boil and allow to simmer for 2 minutes.
- Remove the seafood and vegetables and keep warm.
- Reduce the stock, add the cream and Noilly Prat and allow to reduce a little.
- Return the seafood and vegetables to the sauce.
- Add the raw oysters and their water and the basil to the sauce.
- Monté with butter and season to taste with salt and pepper and cayenne.
- Arrange in small porcelain cocottes and serve immediately.

Note Different seafood may be used, depending upon the season.

Nouilles vertes aux fruits-de-mer
Green noodles with seafood

Ingredients (for 4 people)

320g	(11oz)	green noodles
30g	(1¼oz)	scampi, without shells
60g	(2½oz)	sole fillets, cut into strips
30g	(1¼oz)	scallops, cut in half

▶

30g	(1¼oz)	prawns, without shells
60g	(2½oz)	mussels, without shells
		herbs (dill, basil, parsley)
		lemon juice
		salt, freshly ground pepper
5g	(¼oz)	finely chopped shallot
2cl	(¾fl oz)	olive oil
1cl	(½fl oz)	Cognac
20cl	(6fl oz)	white wine
40cl	(¾ pint)	double cream
40g	(1½oz)	lobster butter (see recipe 35)
30g	(1¼oz)	butter
40g	(1½oz)	Parmesan cheese, grated

Method
- Cook the green noodles *al dente* in salted water.
- Marinate the seafood in chopped herbs, lemon juice, salt and pepper.
- Sweat the finely chopped shallot in olive oil.
- Add the scampi, fillets of sole and scallops, flame with the Cognac and allow to simmer for 2 minutes.
- Add the prawns, mussels and white wine.
- Remove the seafood from the stock and keep warm.
- Reduce the stock, add the cream and reduce until the required consistency is achieved.
- Return the seafood to the sauce and monté with lobster butter.
- Season with salt, freshly ground pepper and finish with lemon juice.
- Sauté the noodles in butter, arrange them on a dish and add the seafood and sauce.
- Serve grated cheese separately.

Coquilles St. Jacques au beurre blanc
Scallops in butter sauce

Ingredients (for 4 people)

16		large scallops in their shells approximately 480g (17oz) net salt, freshly ground pepper
15cl	(¼ pint)	white wine a little lemon juice
10g	(½oz)	finely chopped shallot
100g	(4oz)	butter
5g	(¼oz)	chives, finely chopped

Method

- Open the scallops with a strong knife and lay on the warm hotplate for a few minutes until they open completely. Remove the scallops and roes with a soup spoon. Carefully separate the scallops from the roes and wash thoroughly.
- Halve the scallops and lay on a cloth to dry.
- Poach the seasoned scallops and roes in the white wine and lemon juice in a sauteuse for approximately 1 minute.
- Remove the scallops and roes and keep warm.
- Add the shallot to the stock and reduce to half.
- Allow to cool a little and monté with the soft butter.
- Season the sauce and strain on to warmed plates.
- Arrange the scallops and roes on top and garnish with the chives.

Coquilles St. Jacques à la crème de ciboulette
Scallops in chive sauce

Ingredients (for 4 people)

16		large scallops in their shells (approximately 480g (17oz) net)
2g		finely chopped shallot
10g	(½oz)	butter
10cl	(4fl oz)	dry white wine
10cl	(4fl oz)	vegetable stock (see recipe 13)
10cl	(4fl oz)	double cream
80g	(3¼oz)	butter, to finish
5g	(¼oz)	purée of chives
		salt, freshly ground pepper
		a little chives, finely cut as garnish

Method

- Open the scallops with a strong knife and place on a warm hotplate for a few minutes to open them completely.
- Remove the scallops and roe with a soup spoon.
- Separate the scallops from the roe and wash thoroughly.
- Sweat the chopped shallot in butter and then add the white wine.
- Place the seasoned scallops in the liquid and allow to simmer for no longer than 1 minute, otherwise they will become dry and tough.
- Add the roes at the end.
- Remove from the stock and keep warm.
- Add the vegetable stock and cream and reduce to the required consistency.
- Gradually add the soft butter and purée of chives and season with salt and pepper.
- Pour the sauce on to a suitable dish and arrange the scallops on top. ▶

- Garnish with finely chopped chives. Lay the roes on top.

Coquilles St. Jacques au safran
Scallops with saffron sauce

Ingredients (for 4 people)

16		large scallops in their shells (approximately 480g (17oz) net)
5g	(¼oz)	chopped shallot
20g	(¾oz)	butter
		salt, freshly ground pepper
10cl	(4fl oz)	fish stock (see recipe 6)
10cl	(4fl oz)	white wine
30cl	(½ pint)	double cream
		a few saffron shreds
60g	(2½oz)	diced tomatoes
		chopped parsley

Method

- Open the scallops with a sharp knife and lay on the warm hotplate for a few minutes until they open completely. Remove the scallops and roes with a soup spoon. Carefully separate the scallops from the roes and wash thoroughly.
- Halve the scallops and lay on a cloth to dry.
- Sweat the chopped shallot in butter in a sauté pan without letting it brown.
- Add the seasoned scallops and roes, pour in the fish stock and white wine and allow to simmer for 1 minute.
- Remove the scallops and keep them hot.
- Reduce the stock, add the cream and saffron and reduce to the required consistency.
- Add the tomatoes and parsley and season with salt and pepper.
- Return the scallops and roes to the sauce and serve.

PLATE 11
Above: Tronçon de turbot soufflé aux
écrivisses. Turbot soufflé with crayfish *(Recipe 87).*

Left: Coquilles St.Jacques Galloises.
Scallops fried in butter with leeks
(Recipe 56).

PLATE 12 *(Overleaf)*
Mignons de boeuf aux échallottes.
Mignons of beef with red wine sauce
and chopped shallots *(Recipe 120).*

Scampi sautés Maître Cola
Scampi sautéd with artichokes

In 1969-1970 Mr Cola was sous-chef in the Palace Hotel, St. Moritz. A chef by vocation, he was 65 years old. The head chef, Monsieur de France, was 87 at the time. Fantastic cooking! Truffles and foie gras were used in great quantities. On New Year's Eve alone 45 kilos of caviar were sold. It was an exceptional experience for me to have worked in this world-famous hotel.

Ingredients (for 4 people)

2.4kg	(5¼lb)	scampi with their shells (approximately 600g (1¼lb) net)
		salt, freshly ground pepper
5g	(¼oz)	finely chopped shallot
20g	(¾oz)	butter
2cl		Cognac
20cl	(6fl oz)	white wine
20cl	(6fl oz)	lobster sauce (see recipe 23)
30cl	(½ pint)	double cream
20g	(¾oz)	basil butter (see recipe 33)
2		medium-sized fillets of sole, cut into strips
1		egg
		a few white breadcrumbs
2		artichoke bottoms cut into 4 pieces (see pages 255-6)
10cl	(4fl oz)	oil for deep frying

Method
- Remove the shells from the scampi.
- Add the seasoned scampi to the shallot which has been sweated in butter.
- Sweat briefly and flame with the Cognac.
- Add the white wine, cover and allow to simmer for 1-2 minutes.
- Remove the scampi and keep them warm.
- Reduce the stock, add the lobster sauce and cream and reduce to the required consistency. ▶

- Gradually work in the basil butter and season with salt and pepper.
- Arrange the scampi on a round dish and cover with the sauce.
- Garnish with the pieces of sole which should, in the meantime, have been egg-and-breadcrumbed and deep fried, and the heated artichokes.

Scampi amoureuse
Scampi with Pernod sauce

Ingredients (for 4 people)

600g	(1¼lb)	scampi without their shells
		salt, freshly ground pepper
30g	(1¼oz)	butter
5g	(¼oz)	finely chopped shallot
2cl	(¾fl oz)	Pernod
10cl	(4fl oz)	dry white wine
10cl	(4fl oz)	fish stock (see recipe 6)
30cl	(½ pint)	double cream
		a few chopped tarragon leaves
60g	(2½oz)	butter, to finish

Method

- Sauté the seasoned scampi in butter and finely chopped shallot.
- Flame with Pernod.
- Put in the white wine, cover and allow to simmer for 2-3 minutes.
- Remove the scampi and keep warm.
- Reduce the white wine and then add the fish stock.
- Reduce to half the original volume, then add the cream and tarragon leaves.
- Reduce to the required consistency.
- Mix in the soft butter and season to taste with salt and pepper.

Terrine de tourteau à l'oseille
Terrine of crabmeat with sorrel sauce

Ingredients (for 4 people)

250g	(9oz)	crab flesh, net 2 crabs weighing 800-900g (1½-2lb)
10g	(½oz)	finely chopped shallot
10g	(½oz)	butter
10cl	(4fl oz)	dry white wine
200g	(7oz)	mousseline of pike (see recipe 14)
2cl	(¾fl oz)	Armagnac
		salt, freshly ground pepper

Method

- Wash the crabs and simmer for 5 minutes in boiling salted water, then cool by putting the stock and crab on ice.
- Carefully break open the crabs and remove the crab meat.
- Sweat the chopped shallot in butter until soft, without browning it.
- Add the white wine and reduce, strain and mix with the mousseline of pike.
- Add the crab meat taken from the shell to the mousseline and flavour with Armagnac, salt and pepper.
- Place everything in a greased mould and poach in the oven in a bain-marie for approximately 30 minutes.
- Turn out and cut into 1.5cm (½-¾in) thick slices and serve on the sauce.

Sauce

20cl	(6fl oz)	fish stock (see recipe 6)
10cl	(4fl oz)	white wine
10cl	(4fl oz)	Noilly Prat
10g	(½oz)	finely chopped shallot
30cl	(½ pint)	double cream

►

Recipe 111

a little sorrel cut into strips,
salt, freshly ground pepper
cayenne

Method
- Reduce the fish stock, white wine, Noilly Prat and chopped shallot to half their original volume.
- Add the cream and reduce until the required consistency is achieved.
- Strain through a fine sieve.
- Add the freshly chopped uncooked sorrel and season to taste with salt, pepper and cayenne.

Écrevisses au gratin
Crayfish tails gratinated with hollandaise sauce

Ingredients (for 4 people)

48		crayfish (live)
2 litres	(3½ pints)	water for poaching
1		bouquet garni with tarragon, parsley and dill
20g	(¾oz)	crayfish butter (see recipe 35)
4cl	(1½fl oz)	Cognac
40cl	(¾ pint)	double cream
5cl	(2fl oz)	hollandaise sauce (see recipe 26)
		salt, freshly ground pepper

Method
- Poach the crayfish in boiling salted water with the bouquet garni and the herbs for 2 minutes.
- Break off the crayfish tails and keep warm.
- Warm the crayfish butter, quickly sauté the crayfish in it and flame with Cognac.
- Add two thirds of the cream and bring to the boil.
- Remove the crayfish from the sauce and arrange in a suitable dish.

▶

- Reduce the sauce to the required consistency.
- Add the hollandaise sauce to the sauce and beat in the rest of the cream.
- Adjust the seasoning, pour over the crayfish tails and glaze in the oven or under the grill.

Note It is important to poach the crayfish for only 1 minute so that they are still half raw, otherwise they will become tough. The crayfish tails can be used for the crayfish butter.

Cassolette de moules au fenouil
Mussels in fennel sauce

Ingredients (for 4 people)

2kg	(4½lb)	mussels
5g	(¼oz)	finely chopped shallot
30g	(1¼oz)	butter
20cl	(6fl oz)	dry white wine
100g	(4oz)	finely cut fennel
10cl	(4fl oz)	court-bouillon (see recipe 7)
30cl	(½ pint)	double cream
60g	(2½oz)	butter, to finish
		salt, freshly ground pepper, cayenne a little finely cut chives and fennel leaves

Method
- Scrape the mussels clean, brush them and wash thoroughly.
- Sweat the shallot well in butter, add the mussels.
- Add the white wine, fennel and court-bouillon, cover and bring to the boil. ▶

- Strain the stock and reduce.
- Meanwhile take the mussels out of their shells, remove the beards and keep them warm.
- Add cream to the reduced stock and reduce until the required consistency is achieved.
- Gradually add the soft butter.
- Return the mussels to the sauce and season with salt, pepper and cayenne.
- Add the chives and fennel leaves.
- Arrange in a cassolette and serve immediately.

Brioche navigateur
Brioche with seafood and mushrooms

Ingredients (for 4 people)

4		brioches of about 8cm (2¾in) diameter (see recipe 17)
2g		finely chopped shallot
20g	(¾oz)	butter
		salt, freshly ground pepper
220g	(8oz)	monk fish, filleted and cut into strips of approximately 10g (½oz)
1		sole, approximately 500g (18oz), filleted and cut into strips of approximately 10g (½oz)
8		scampi, without their shells
4		scallops, cut in half
50g	(2oz)	small mushrooms
20cl	(6fl oz)	white wine
10cl	(4fl oz)	Sherry
20cl	(6fl oz)	lobster sauce (see recipe 23)
30cl	(½ pint)	double cream
10cl	(4fl oz)	hollandaise sauce (see recipe 26)

Method
- Hollow out the centres of the brioches and keep the tops. ▶

- Sweat the chopped shallot in butter without browning it.
- Add the seasoned pieces of monk fish and continue to sweat.
- Add the seasoned sole, scampi, scallops and mushrooms and sweat, then put in the white wine and Sherry.
- Cover and poach for 2-3 minutes.
- Strain the stock and reduce.
- Add the lobster sauce and cream and reduce until the required consistency is achieved.
- Return the sea food to the sauce, bring to the boil and taste. Season with salt and pepper.
- Fill the hollowed out warm brioches with the mixture, cover with hollandaise sauce and briefly glaze.
- Put on the lids of the brioches and serve immediately.

Chapter 8

Meat Dishes

Meat Dishes

Meat

The quality of meat depends greatly upon the condition of the animals when they are slaughtered. Stiffness occurs when animals which are not used to moving are taken to the place of slaughter. Many animals become tired even after a small amount of effort. Their flesh is dark in colour and has a sticky, rubber-like quality. This defect can even be seen in young cattle. In professional jargon, this is called 'dark firm dry'. This defect can be overcome by the physical training of the animals to be slaughtered, a protective form of transport and long rests before slaughter in conjunction with fodder containing sugar. Such procedures, however, are limited because of the cost element which makes it uneconomic.

Meat should never be cut haphazardly. There is connective tissue lying between each muscle which makes it easier to separate the various parts. In this way stored-up subcutaneous fatty layers and sinews can be removed without difficulty. The remaining pieces are compact muscles with even fibrillation. Meat becomes 'sticky' if dampness appearing on it, or dampness which comes from elsewhere, is not allowed to dry. Therefore, meat must be kept away from steam and from products which produce steam.

Beef

Young first class beef should be red in colour, but not too dark. As the sign of a completed fattening time the kidney should be 'covered', i.e. it should be covered with a thick layer of fat, not too yellow in colour. An indication of a proper fattening which has not been effected too quickly is 'marbled' meat — roasting beef with fatty veins running through it. The meat should be stored for approximately fifteen to twenty-one days before use.

Veal

If a calf is properly fattened, i.e. is fed only on milk, it will have a pinkish white flesh. The kidney should be completely covered in white fat. Meat from calves which are too young and not properly fattened will disintegrate badly during preparation. Veal should be stored eight to ten days before use.

Lamb

Most chefs prefer lamb to pork and beef because it is more tender and has a more pronounced taste of its own. With poultry the experts are in agreement; the best chickens and hens come from the Bresse region of France. With lamb one cannot be so definitive. Nearly every chef has his preferred area, e.g. Ireland or Scotland, Brittany or Normandy. It is a question of the chef's personal preference whether he chooses lamb which has lived on coastal fields and been fed on grass containing sea salt or the animals which have lived in the mountains and been pampered with spicy herbs. Meat from white mountain lambs is available throughout most of the year.

Lambs' meat comes from grazing sheep which are not yet fully grown. The best age is ten months. Milk lambs (which are only available in spring) are animals which are still suckling and not yet grazing. These lambs have white flesh. In order not to overshadow the special taste of lamb all cuts should be prepared as naturally as possible. As with all types of meat, lamb should be stored for a few days. By this means it becomes more tender and improves in taste.

Pork

Good pork is pale pink in colour and slightly marbled. It should never be dark red and watery. It should also hang for five to six days.

Entrecôte sautée Dorchester
Sirloin steak in cream sauce with four different peppers

Ingredients (for 4 people)

4		entrecôte steaks (180g (6oz) each)
		some white and black peppercorns, well crushed
5cl	(2fl oz)	peanut oil
4cl	(1½fl oz)	Cognac
20cl	(7fl oz)	brown veal stock (see recipe 4)
20cl	(7fl oz)	double cream
40g	(1½oz)	butter, to finish
3g		green peppercorns
3g		pink peppercorns
		salt, freshly ground pepper

Method

- Season the well trimmed entrecôtes with white and black peppercorns and salt.
- Sauté them on both sides in hot oil.
- Remove the entrecôtes and keep warm.
- Remove the fat, flame the cooking juices with Cognac, add the veal stock and reduce to half its original volume.
- Add the cream and reduce to the required consistency.
- Monté with butter and season with salt and pepper.

- Add the green and pink peppercorns just before serving.
- Cover the entrecôtes with the sauce.

Note It is best to add the green and pink peppercorns right at the end, otherwise the sauce will be too spicy.

Coeur de filet de boeuf soufflé

Fillet of beef with chicken mousseline and Madeira sauce

Ingredients (for 4 people)

4		beef fillets (160g (5½oz) each)
		salt, freshly ground pepper
2cl	(¾fl oz)	peanut oil
4		slices of goose liver, 15g (½oz) each
120g	(4½oz)	chicken mousseline (see recipe 15)
1		small piece crépine
20cl	(6fl oz)	Madeira sauce (see recipe 30)

Method

- Season the well trimmed beef fillets and sauté them quickly on one side in the oil.
- Lay a slice of goose liver on the side which has been fried and spread with the chicken mousseline. Put each in the crépine.
- Place the fillets in a suitable sautoir and cook in a moderate oven according to taste.
- Arrange, cover with the Madeira sauce and serve immediately.

Célestine de boeuf au poivre vert
Strips of beef in cream sauce with green peppercorns

Ingredients (for 4 people)

640g	(1¼lb)	beef fillet, well trimmed and cut into thin strips
2cl	(¾fl oz)	peanut oil
2cl	(¾fl oz)	Cognac
10g	(½oz)	finely chopped shallot
15cl	(¼ pint)	red wine
30cl	(½ pint)	brown veal stock (see recipe 4)
20cl	(7fl oz)	double cream
50g	(2oz)	butter, to finish
5g	(¼oz)	green peppercorns
		salt, freshly ground pepper

Method

- Season the pieces of fillet and sauté them rare in the hot oil.
- Flame with the Cognac.
- Discard the fat and remove the meat from the pan.
- Add the finely chopped shallot and red wine and reduce.
- Add the brown veal stock and reduce to half its original volume.
- Put in the cream and monté with butter.
- Remove the sauce from the heat, add the green peppercorns and season with salt and pepper.
- Mix the meat with the sauce and serve immediately.

Rosette de boeuf
Grand Hôtel

*Fillet of beef with meat marrow
and red wine sauce*

Ingredients (for 4 people)

4		tournedos (160g (5½oz) each)
		salt, freshly ground pepper
1cl	(½fl oz)	peanut oil

Garnish

100g	(4oz)	meat marrow, diced
		sprinkling of chopped parsley
10g	(½oz)	white breadcrumbs
5cl	(2fl oz)	white wine
4		blanched marrow bones
		(approximately 1cm (½in) high)

Method

- Season the well trimmed tournedos and grill according to taste. Keep warm.
- Mix well together the meat marrow, parsley, breadcrumbs and white wine.
- Arrange this garnish on the tournedos and glaze in the oven with the heat coming from above for 6-7 minutes.
- Arrange the tournedos on the marrow bones and serve with red wine sauce (see recipe 119).

Note Serving the tournedos on the marrow bones is not only original but it also prevents the meat from becoming overcooked on a hot serving dish.

Sauce au vin rouge
Red wine sauce

Ingredients (for 4 people)

10g	(½oz)	finely chopped shallot
5g	(¼oz)	butter
30cl	(½ pint)	red wine (Aloxe Corton)
		a little thyme
30cl	(½ pint)	brown veal stock (see recipe 4)
40g	(1½oz)	butter, to finish
		salt, freshly ground white pepper

Method
- Sweat the finely chopped shallot carefully in butter, without giving it any colour.
- Add the red wine.
- Put in the thyme and reduce to half the original volume.
- Add the veal stock and reduce again.
- Monté with butter.
- Season with salt and pepper.

Mignons de boeuf aux échalotes
Mignons of beef with red wine sauce and chopped shallots

Ingredients (for 4 people)

8		mignons of beef well trimmed (80g (3oz) each)
		salt
		freshly ground pepper
4cl	(1½fl oz)	peanut oil

▶

15g	(½oz)	butter
40g	(1½oz)	finely chopped shallots
15cl	(¼ pint)	red wine
30cl	(½ pint)	brown veal stock (see recipe 4)
40g	(1½oz)	butter to finish

Method (See Plate 12)
- Season the well trimmed fillet mignons with salt and pepper.
- Sauté them on both sides in hot oil.
- Remove the mignons and keep warm.
- Remove the fat, add the butter and sweat the chopped shallots without giving any colour.
- Add the red wine and reduce.
- Add the brown veal stock and reduce to the required consistency.
- Monté with butter and season with salt and pepper.
- Cover the mignons with the sauce and serve immediately.

Côte de boeuf marinée aux herbes du jardin
Grilled rib of beef with herbs and butter sauce

Ingredients (for 4 people)

1		beef cutlet (1.4kg (3lb))

Marinade

10cl	(4fl oz)	olive oil
1		small sprig of thyme
1		small sprig of rosemary
4		sage leaves
8		basil leaves
		a little garlic

►

salt
coarsely crushed black pepper
a little watercress

30cl   (½ pint)   Foyot sauce (see recipe 31)
a little meat extract (see recipe 9)

Method (See Plate 13)
- Marinate the well trimmed beef cutlet for 12 hours in the olive oil, thyme, rosemary, sage, basil and garlic.
- Season with salt and coarsely crushed pepper and then grill.
- Arrange on a suitable dish.
- Garnish with a sprig of rosemary sautéd in butter (to give it more taste) and some watercress.
- Garnish the Sauce Foyot with meat extract and serve separately.

Note It is important that when the beef is being marinated it is turned frequently. To prevent the meat juices running out, the beef should rest for 10 minutes before being cut.

Gigot d'agneau farci en croûte
Stuffed leg of lamb in pastry

Ingredients (for 4 people)

1		leg of lamb (1.5kg (3lb))
200g	(7oz)	lambs' kidneys with fat, skin and nerves removed
		salt, freshly ground pepper
1g		herb mixture (see recipe 123)
20g	(¾oz)	butter
2cl	(¾fl oz)	Madeira
1		clove of garlic
2cl	(¾fl oz)	olive oil

►

250g	(9oz)	puff pastry (see recipe 19)
1		egg yolk

Method

- Remove the two main bones from the leg of lamb without cutting into the meat and trim well.
- Cut the lambs' kidneys in half, season with salt, pepper and herb mixture.
- Sauté quickly in butter (until pink).
- Remove the kidneys from the pan, discard the butter, add the Madeira, allow to reduce a little and then return the kidneys to the pan.
- Garnish the leg of lamb with garlic and stuff with the cooled kidneys.
- Bind the meat carefully to give it a good shape.
- Season with salt and pepper and roast on all sides in olive oil in a suitable dish in the oven.
- Lay on a grid and allow to cool.
- Remove the string and pack the meat carefully in the puff pastry.
- Brush with egg yolk and bake for 20-25 minutes at an even very hot temperature (approximately 230°C (450°F)).

Note After baking it is important that the gigot is allowed to rest in a fairly warm place for 10 minutes. This will prevent the meat juices from running out when it is cut.

Mélange d'aromats
Herb mixture

Ingredients

50g	(2oz)	thyme
30g	(1¼oz)	pepper herb
25g	(1oz)	rosemary
10g	(½oz)	garlic, finely chopped

▶

25g	(1oz)	tarragon
20g	(¾oz)	marjoram
5g	(¼oz)	sage
20g	(¾oz)	parsley

Method
- Remove the stalks from all the herbs and chop finely.
- Use only fresh herbs.

Mignons d'agneau au Porto
Mignons of lamb with Port wine sauce

Ingredients (for 4 people)

8		pieces of lamb mignon, weighing 70g (2¾oz) each (cut from the saddle) salt, freshly ground pepper
30g	(1¼oz)	butter
15g	(½oz)	finely chopped shallot
5cl	(2fl oz)	Port
10cl	(4fl oz)	brown veal stock (see recipe 4)
15cl	(¼ pint)	double cream
50g	(2oz)	butter, to finish

Method
- Bind each well trimmed lamb mignon with a small piece of string.
- Season with salt and freshly ground pepper.
- Heat the butter in a suitable pan and sauté the lamb mignons on both sides.
- Add the finely chopped shallot, cover and allow to simmer for 2 to 3 minutes at a moderate heat.
- Remove the string from the meat and keep the meat warm.
- Remove the butter, add the port to the meat juices, then add the brown veal stock and reduce. ▶

- Add the cream, bring to the boil and monté with butter.
- Strain the sauce through a fine sieve or muslin, season with salt and pepper.
- Arrange the lamb mignons on the spinach (see recipe 125) and cover with the sauce.

Épinards en feuilles
Leaf spinach

Ingredients (for 4 people)

200g	(7oz)	young spinach, without stalks
5g	(¼oz)	finely chopped shallot
1		garlic clove with skin
20g	(¾oz)	butter
		salt, freshly ground pepper
		nutmeg

Method
- Wash the spinach leaves well and dry.
- Sweat the finely chopped shallot and the whole garlic clove carefully in butter, without giving them any colour.
- Add the spinach leaves and sweat well.
- Season with salt, freshly ground pepper and nutmeg.
- Remove the clove of garlic before serving and use elsewhere.

Selle d'agneau pochée aux légumes

Poached saddle of lamb with vegetables

Ingredients (for 4 people)

600g	(1¼lb)	saddle of lamb, without bones
30cl	(½ pint)	white veal stock (see recipe 2)
30cl	(½ pint)	lamb stock (see recipe 5)
50g	(2oz)	butter
80g	(3¼oz)	onions } peeled, quartered
80g	(3¼oz)	red onions } and broken up
150g	(5oz)	white leek, cut into diagonal slices
140g	(4¾oz)	Savoy cabbage leaves, roughly chopped
100g	(4oz)	small Brussels sprouts, divided into individual leaves
		a little finely chopped parsley, chives and basil
		salt, freshly ground pepper

Method

- Skin and trim the lamb. Cut into pieces.
- Boil up the veal and lamb stock and allow to reduce a little.
- Carefully monté with the soft butter.
- Quickly blanch the onions, leek, cabbage and Brussels sprouts in boiling salted water.
- Remove and allow to drain.
- Add the pieces of lamb to the stock and allow to simmer for 10 minutes.
- Remove the meat and allow to rest on a grid.
- Return the blanched vegetables to the stock and bring to the boil.
- Add the meat.
- Add the freshly chopped parsley, chives and basil and season with salt and pepper. ▶

- Remove the vegetables and arrange in a suitable dish.
- Just before serving, cut the meat into pieces
- approximately 1cm (under ½in) thick and arrange on the vegetables.
- Serve immediately.

Note To give this dish a special taste, an unpeeled garlic clove may be poached with it, which does not bring out the taste of the garlic too much.

Blanquette d'agneau au safran
Blanquette of lamb with saffron sauce

Ingredients (for 4 people)

800g	(1¾lb)	lamb (breast and shoulder)
60cl	(1 pint)	lamb stock well seasoned (see recipe 5)
10cl	(4fl oz)	white wine
150g	(5oz)	bouquet garni (onions, carrots, celery, ¼ bay leaf, clove, some parsley stalks)
		some saffron stigmas
2		egg yolks
30cl	(½ pint)	double cream
50g	(2oz)	butter, to finish
1cl	(½fl oz)	lemon juice
		salt, freshly ground pepper

Garnish

50g	(2oz)	turned carrots
50g	(2oz)	turned turnips
50g	(2oz)	fine green beans
		all above cooked in salted water until crisp
30g	(1¼oz)	glazed pearl onions ▶

Recipes 126 & 127

Method
- Trim the meat well and cut into pieces weighing 40g (1½oz) each.
- Blanch in salt water, cool and wash.
- Place the meat in a suitable pan, add the lamb stock and white wine.
- Bring to the boil and skim.
- Add the bouquet garni and saffron leaves and simmer until the meat is tender, occasionally removing the fat and skimming.
- Remove the cooked meat, strain the stock through a fine sieve and reduce to half its original volume.
- Mix the egg yolks with the cream and add to the stock.
- Strain the bound sauce through a fine muslin and carefully monté with butter.
- Add the lemon juice and season with salt and pepper.
- Arrange the meat on a suitable dish and cover with the sauce.
- Garnish with the carrots, turnips and green beans and the freshly glazed pearl onions.

Note The sauce should not be boiled after binding.

Piccata de veau Cavalieri
Fillet of veal with cheese and green noodles

Ingredients (for 4 people)

12		pieces of veal fillet (30g (1¼oz) each)
		salt, freshly ground white pepper
		a little flour
2		eggs
20g	(¾oz)	grated Parmesan cheese
4cl	(1½fl oz)	olive oil
40g	(1½oz)	butter

►

200g	(7oz)	tomatoes, cut into small dice
80g	(3¼oz)	mozzarella cheese, sliced
2cl	(¾fl oz)	double cream
300g	(10oz)	fresh green noodles (see recipe 22)
30cl	(½ pint)	Madeira sauce (see recipe 30)
20g	(¾oz)	butter, to finish

Method

- Season the thinly cut and flattened veal fillets and dust them with the flour.
- Crack the eggs, mix with the Parmesan cheese and use to coat the veal fillet.
- Sauté until golden brown in the olive oil and butter.
- Drain the tomatoes of most of their juice, season them and sauté in butter. Arrange on the veal.
- Lay the mozzarella cheese on the tomatoes, sprinkle with the cream and melt the cheese under the grill.
- Carefully season with salt and pepper.
- Cook the noodles *al dente*, then arrange the meat on them.
- Finish the Madeira sauce with butter and serve separately.

Note It is advisable to prepare the noodles freshly for use in this dish.

Mignons de veau à l'oseille
Mignons of veal in cream sauce and sorrel

Ingredients (for 4 people)

12		veal mignons (50g (2oz) each) salt, freshly ground pepper
2cl	(¾fl oz)	peanut oil
20g	(¾oz)	butter
4cl	(1½fl oz)	white veal stock (see recipe 2)

▶

Method

- · Season the veal mignons and sauté in the peanut oil and butter until light brown on both sides.
- Remove the meat and keep warm.
- Discard the fat.
- Add the white veal stock to the cooking juices and reduce to half the original volume (reserve for adding to the sauce later).

Sauce

10g	(½oz)	butter
2g		finely chopped shallot
40g	(1½oz)	diced tomato
5cl	(2fl oz)	white wine
3cl	(1fl oz)	Noilly Prat
20cl	(6fl oz)	white veal stock (see recipe 2)
15cl	(¼ pint)	double cream
40g	(1½oz)	butter, to finish
20g	(¾oz)	sorrel, cut into strips approximately 3mm (⅛in) thick salt, freshly ground pepper

Method

- Sweat the finely chopped shallot in the butter.
- Add the diced tomato and sweat well.
- Add the white wine and Noilly Prat and reduce.
- Add the white veal stock and reduce again.
- Add the cream, bring to the boil and pass through a fine sieve.
- Add the reserved cooking juices to the sauce and monté with butter.
- Add the sorrel and season with salt and pepper.
- Cover a suitable dish with the sauce, place the veal on top and serve immediately.

Médaillons de veau à l'orange et au citron
Medallions of veal with oranges and lemons

Ingredients (for 4 people)

8		veal medallions (70g (2¾oz) each)
		salt, freshly ground white pepper
40g	(1½oz)	butter
10cl	(4fl oz)	white wine
20cl	(6fl oz)	brown veal stock (see recipe 4)
30cl	(½ pint)	cream
		a little orange and lemon juice
8		small slices of peeled orange
8		small slices of peeled lemon
		a little grated orange and lemon zest (blanched)

Method

- Sauté the seasoned medallions in butter until golden brown.
- Remove the meat and keep hot; discard the butter.
- Add the white wine to the meat juices, then the stock and reduce.
- Add the cream and reduce to the required consistency.
- Add the orange and lemon juice then season the sauce with salt and pepper.
- Arrange the meat, and pour the sauce over it.
- Garnish each medallion with one slice of orange and one slice of lemon.
- Just before serving garnish with the orange and lemon zest.

Côte de veau sautée aux morilles farcies

Veal cutlets with stuffed morels

Ingredients (for 4 people)

4		veal cutlets (180g (6oz) each)
		salt, freshly ground white pepper
20g	(¾oz)	butter
10cl	(4fl oz)	Port
40cl	(¾ pint)	brown veal stock (see recipe 4)
40g	(1½oz)	butter to finish

Method

- Season the well trimmed cutlets and sauté carefully in butter.
- Remove the cutlets, discard the butter and add the Port.
- Add the brown veal stock and reduce to the required consistency.
- Gradually add the butter and season with salt and pepper.
- Garnish with stuffed morels (see recipe 132) and serve immediately.

Morilles farcies
Stuffed morels

Ingredients (for 4 people)

12		medium sized fresh morels
40g	(1½oz)	veal brain
		salt, freshly ground pepper
		a little lemon juice
20g	(¾oz)	white breadcrumbs
2cl	(¾fl oz)	cream, for soaking the breadcrumbs
20g	(¾oz)	young spinach, without stalks
10g	(½oz)	sorrel leaves, without stalks
		some chervil leaves
10g	(½oz)	watercress
60g	(2½oz)	chicken mousseline (see recipe 15)

Stock

10cl	(4fl oz)	strong white poultry stock
		(see recipe 1)
10cl	(4fl oz)	Madeira
2cl	(¾fl oz)	Noilly Prat
		salt, freshly ground pepper

Method

- Clean the morels and wash them through several times (do not soak in water).
- Dry on a cloth.
- Remove the skin from the well soaked brain.
- Poach in lightly salted water with a little lemon juice and allow to cool in the stock.
- Remove the brain from the stock and dry on a cloth.
- Moisten the breadcrumbs in lukewarm cream.
- Finely chop the blanched spinach and sorrel leaves, chervil and watercress.
- Add to these the chicken mousseline, the soaked breadcrumbs and coarsely chopped brain, mix well together and season well with salt and pepper. ▶

Recipe 132

- Stuff the morels with this farce, using a piping bag.
- Carefully poach in the stock for about 15 to 20 minutes.

Note The stuffed morels may be served with various meat dishes.

Emincé de veau belle forestière
Strips of veal in cream sauce with mixed mushrooms

Ingredients (for 4 people)

600g	(1¼lb)	veal fillet, cut in slices
		salt, freshly ground white pepper
20g	(¾oz)	butter
20cl	(6fl oz)	white wine
20cl	(6fl oz)	brown veal stock (see recipe 4)
30cl	(½ pint)	double cream
50g	(2oz)	small chanterelles
50g	(2oz)	yellow boletus (cèpes)
50g	(2oz)	mushrooms
2g		finely chopped shallot
		chopped parsley
30g	(1¼oz)	butter to finish

Method
- Carefully sauté the seasoned meat in butter without browning it.
- Let the meat drain through a sieve.
- Add the white wine to the meat juices, allow to reduce a little and then add the veal stock. Bring to the boil and add the cream.
- Reduce until the required consistency is achieved.

▶

- Thoroughly wash the chanterelles, wash and slice the yellow boletus and mushrooms. Sweat with the remaining butter and chopped shallot.
- Add the sautéd meat, mushrooms and the chopped parsley to the sauce, monté with hard butter, season with salt and pepper and serve immediately.

Filet de veau poêlé au foie gras
Fillet of veal with goose liver

Ingredients (for 4 people)

1		veal fillet, (about 600g (1¼lb)) well trimmed salt, freshly ground pepper
60g	(2½oz)	barding lard
2cl	(¾fl oz)	peanut oil
20g	(¾oz)	butter
25g	(1oz)	diced carrot
25g	(1oz)	diced onion
25g	(1oz)	diced celery
20cl	(6fl oz)	white wine
30cl	(½ pint)	brown veal stock (see recipe 4)
20cl	(6fl oz)	cream
40g	(1½oz)	butter, to finish
80g	(3¼oz)	goose liver, thinly sliced
60g	(2½oz)	raw ham, thinly sliced

Method

- Season the veal fillet well, cover with barding lard and sauté in the oil until golden brown.
- Sweat the vegetables in butter and arrange in a suitable pan.
- Add the meat and sauté in a moderate oven for 15-18 minutes with the white wine and veal stock, basting continuously. ▶

- Remove the fillet and keep warm.
- Reduce the stock, add the cream and reduce until the required consistency is achieved.
- Pass through a sieve, monté with butter and season.
- Cut the fillet into slices — without the barding lard — and place the slices of goose liver, which have been wrapped in raw ham and sautéd, between the fillet slices.
- Cover a suitable dish with the sauce and dress the meat on top.

Ris de veau aux feuilles d'épinards
Calves' sweetbreads with spinach

Ingredients (for 4 people)

600g	(1¼lb)	fresh sweetbreads
15g	(½oz)	butter
100g	(4oz)	carrots, sliced
50g	(2oz)	finely chopped onion
10g	(½oz)	finely chopped shallot
1		clove of garlic, unpeeled
1		small sprig of thyme
1		bay leaf
		salt, freshly ground pepper
10cl	(4fl oz)	Noilly Prat
25cl	(8fl oz)	double cream
40g	(1½oz)	sorrel, coarsely chopped
50g	(2oz)	butter, to finish
100g	(4oz)	fresh young spinach, blanched

Method
- Blanch the well soaked sweetbreads, cool immediately and trim well.

PLATE 13
Côte de boeuf marinée aux herbes du jardin. (Grilled rib of beef with herbs and butter sauce) Recipe 121.

Recipes 134 & 135

►

- Butter the bottom of a pan and spread with the carrots, finely chopped onion and shallot.
- Lay the sweetbreads on top.
- Season with the garlic, thyme, bay leaf, salt and pepper.
- Cover and steam slowly in their own juice in the oven.
- Remove the sweetbreads and keep warm, add the Noilly Prat and allow to reduce a little.
- Add the cream, bring to the boil and pass through a fine sieve.
- Add the sorrel and simmer gently for 2 to 3 minutes.
- Very gradually add the butter to the sauce and season well with salt and pepper.
- Cut the sweetbreads into even slices.
- Arrange the sauce on a suitable dish with the sweetbreads on top.
- Sweat the spinach in butter, season with salt and pepper and use as garnish.

Ris de veau piqués à la vapeur
Steamed calves' sweetbreads with truffles, vegetables and cream sauce

Ingredients (for 4 people)

700g	(1½lb)	fresh sweetbreads
30cl	(½ pint)	white veal stock well seasoned (see recipe 2)
40g	(1½oz)	onion
20g	(¾oz)	carrot
30g	(1¼oz)	leek
20g	(¾oz)	celery
1		small bay leaf
		a little parsley, basil leaves

onion, carrot, leek, celery } diced

PLATE 14
Foie de veau vénitienne. (Calves' liver with onions and Madeira sauce) Recipe 139.

► Recipes 135 & 136

60g	(2½oz)	ham, cut into thick strips
10g	(½oz)	black truffles, cut roughly into julienne strips
10cl	(4fl oz)	white wine
10cl	(4fl oz)	Sherry
30g	(1¼oz)	butter, to finish
		salt and freshly ground white pepper

Method

- Soak the sweetbreads for several hours in water, changing frequently.
- Blanch the sweetbreads and remove the skin.
- Allow the veal stock, diced vegetables, bay leaf, parsley and basil to simmer for 5 minutes.
- Trim the sweetbreads and garnish them with truffles and ham.
- Strain the stock, add the white wine and cook the sweetbreads in the steam.
- Remove the sweetbreads and keep hot.
- Reduce the stock to a third of its original volume, flavour with Sherry and monté with butter.
- Season the sauce with salt and freshly ground pepper.
- Cut the sweetbreads into slices and arrange attractively on the sauce.

Note Young tender spinach sautéd in butter makes a good accompaniment to this dish.

‘If we would foster national happiness, the problem is not with what and how to feed the people. The problem is how to bring the food to the people, and then to see it cooked properly. ’

Rognons de veau au vinaigre de vin

Veal kidneys in red wine vinegar sauce

Ingredients (for 4 people)

4		veal kidneys
		(approximately 140g (4¾oz) each)
		salt, freshly ground pepper
30g	(1¼oz)	butter
30g	(1¼oz)	finely chopped shallots
20cl	(6fl oz)	red wine
5cl	(2fl oz)	red wine vinegar
30cl	(½ pint)	veal stock (see recipe 4)
50g	(2oz)	butter, to finish

Garnish

40g	(1½oz)	carrot ⎫	
40g	(1½oz)	leek ⎬	cut into julienne strips
40g	(1½oz)	celery ⎭	
10g	(½oz)	butter	

Method

- Remove the fat and internal nerve from the kidneys.
- Season the kidneys and sauté in butter, then cover them and continue to brown in the oven for 5-6 minutes.
- Remove the kidneys and keep hot; discard the fat.
- Put a little butter into the pan, add the chopped shallot and sweat.
- Add the red wine and red wine vinegar and reduce well.
- Pour in the veal stock and reduce until the required consistency is obtained.
- Monté with butter and season with salt and pepper.
- Arrange the kidneys in a suitable dish and cover with the sauce.
- Garnish with the julienne of vegetables, sautéd in butter. ▶

Note It is important that the red wine vinegar and the red wine are allowed to reduce sufficiently, otherwise the sauce will taste sour.

Rognons de veau à la moutarde
Veal kidneys in mustard sauce

Ingredients (for 4 people)

4		pieces of veal kidney with a little fat (approximately 140g (5oz) each) salt, freshly ground pepper
30g	(1¼oz)	butter
5cl	(2fl oz)	Calvados
10cl	(4fl oz)	brown veal stock (see recipe 4)
30cl	(½ pint)	double cream
10g	(½oz)	Dijon mustard

Method

- Cut the kidneys into slices approximately 1cm (½in) thick; cut away the internal nerve without removing the fat.
- Sauté the seasoned kidney slices on both sides in butter and then flame with the Calvados.
- Remove the kidneys and keep them hot.
- Add the veal stock and allow to reduce a little.
- Add the cream, bring quickly to the boil, mix in the mustard and season to taste with salt and pepper.
- Arrange the kidneys in a suitable dish and cover with the sauce.

Note It is important that the kidneys be served pink. On no account should the kidneys be boiled in the sauce, otherwise they will toughen.

Foie de veau vénitienne
Calves' liver with onions and Madeira sauce

Ingredients (for 4 people)

600g	(1¼lb)	calves' liver
40g	(1½oz)	butter
100g	(4oz)	onions, finely chopped
20cl	(6fl oz)	Madeira
1		sage leaf, chopped
20cl	(6fl oz)	brown veal stock (see recipe 4)
50g	(2oz)	butter, to finish
		salt, freshly ground pepper

Method (See Plate 14)

- Remove the skin and nerves from the liver.
- Cut into slices, approximately 3cm (1¼in) across.
- Sweat the finely chopped onions in 20g (¾oz) of butter until golden brown, stirring constantly.
- Add 15cl (5fl oz) of the Madeira and the sage leaf and reduce to half its original volume.
- Add the veal stock and reduce to the required consistency.
- Heat 20g (¾oz) of butter in a sauteuse, add the seasoned liver and turn quickly 2 or 3 times.
- Add the liver without the butter to the onions and sauce and gradually work in the soft butter with a spoon over medium heat.
- Finish with the rest of the Madeira and season with salt and pepper.

Note This dish should be served in a small amount of sauce.

Médaillons de filet de porc sauce Western

Fillet of pork medallions with Western sauce

Ingredients (for 4 people)

8		pork fillet medallions, 70g (2¾oz) each (well trimmed) salt, freshly ground white pepper some flour
2cl	(¾fl oz)	olive oil
20g	(¾oz)	butter
4cl	(1½fl oz)	white wine
30cl	(½ pint)	sauce Western (see recipe 25)

Method

- Season the pork medallions with salt and pepper and lightly dust with flour.
- Heat the olive oil and butter gently in a suitable pan.
- Put in the medallions and sauté slowly; remove and keep warm then drain off the fat.
- Add the white wine and allow to reduce.
- Add this stock to the sauce Western.
- Arrange the juicy pork medallions on a suitable dish and cover with the well seasoned sauce.

Mignons de filet de porc au Roquefort
Pork fillets in Roquefort sauce

Ingredients (for 4 people)

8		mignons of pork fillet, weighing 70g (2¾oz) each and well trimmed
		salt, freshly ground pepper
2cl	(¾fl oz)	olive oil
20g	(¾oz)	butter
2		garlic cloves, unpeeled
1		sprig rosemary
40g	(1½oz)	young carrots, cut into sticks
40g	(1½oz)	celery, cut into sticks
50g	(2oz)	haricots verts, thoroughly washed

Sauce

10g	(½oz)	butter
5g	(¼oz)	finely chopped shallot
4cl	(1½fl oz)	dry white wine
3cl	(1fl oz)	cider
10cl	(4fl oz)	brown veal stock (see recipe 4)
5cl	(2fl oz)	double cream
40g	(1½oz)	Roquefort cheese, in small pieces
		salt, freshly ground pepper

Method

- Season the well trimmed mignons of pork with salt and pepper.
- Heat the olive oil and butter in a suitable pan.
- Add the mignons.
- Put in the garlic cloves and sprig of rosemary.
- Sauté the mignons carefully at a moderate heat on both sides without overcooking them.
- Remove the meat and keep warm.
- Discard the fat.
- For the sauce heat the butter in the pan.
- Add the finely chopped shallot and sweat. ▶

- Add the white wine and cider and allow to reduce.
- Add the veal stock and reduce to half its original volume.
- Strain, boil up and add the cream.
- Put in the cheese and season the sauce with salt and pepper.
- Cook the carrots, celery and haricots verts separately in salted water until crisp and add to the sauce.
- Arrange the sauce on a plate with the mignons of pork on top.
- Serve immediately.

Note Walnuts, peeled and sautéd in butter, may be added to this dish to enrich it.

Médaillons de porc aux pruneaux
Medallions of pork with prunes

Ingredients (for 4 people)

8		pork medallions (70g (2¾oz) each) well trimmed, including kidney
8		small prunes, with stones removed
		salt, freshly ground pepper
		some flour
2cl	(¾fl oz)	olive oil
20g	(¾oz)	butter
10cl	(4fl oz)	white wine
15cl	(¼ pint)	brown veal stock (see recipe 4)
30g	(1¼oz)	butter, to finish

Garnish

50g	(2oz)	turned carrots ⎫ cooked
50g	(2oz)	turned turnips ⎭ until crisp
8		small blanched prunes, with stones removed
20g	(¾oz)	butter
		a little chopped parsley

▶

Method

- Arrange the pork medallions on a plate.
- Place the prunes in cold water in a suitable pan, cover and bring to the boil.
- Remove from the heat and allow to simmer for 30 minutes in the water.
- Pour off the water, cut the prunes in half and dry on a cloth.
- Carefully piqué the pork medallions on both sides with the blanched and halved prunes.
- Season with salt and pepper and lightly dust with flour.
- Heat the oil and butter in a sauteuse.
- Put in the pork medallions and slowly sauté on both sides until juicy, constantly using a spoon to baste during the process.
- Remove the medallions from the pan and keep warm.
- Pour off the fat.
- Add the white wine to the pan and reduce a little.
- Add the veal stock and reduce until the required consistency is achieved.
- Strain through a sieve and monté with butter.
- Season with salt and pepper.
- Cover the juicy pork medallions with the sauce.
- Sauté the carrots, turnips and prunes in the butter and arrange on the steaks.
- Garnish with the freshly chopped parsley and serve immediately.

Chapter 9

Poultry Dishes

Poultry Dishes

By poultry we understand the domestic or fattened bird, such as chickens, geese, ducks, turkeys etc. All other types are classed as feathered game.

Poultry meat has the same qualities as other meat. It is generally liked, however, because of its mild pleasant flavour and the white meat of young poultry is well known for being easy to digest. It contains animal protein, fat, vitamins and minerals (iron and phosphorus). A distinction is made between white poultry meat such as chicken, poussin, turkey and dark poultry meat such as duck, guinea-fowl, goose and pigeon. The difference in colour does not affect the quality.

Young poultry is pre-eminent in a good kitchen. The signs of young poultry are: white fattened poultry — a breast bone which is pliable and not ossified, strong legs, claws which are not worn down, bright red crest, supple skin on legs. Dark fattened poultry — if the windpipe is soft and flexible then the bird is still young, otherwise it is old. With geese and ducks the same thing can be seen from the tip of the breast bone. However that is more difficult to test in these birds because the body is covered with fat and therefore does not yield very much to the pressure of a finger.

In England there is not quite the degree of difference between various types of chicken as there is on the continent. In fact chickens range from the baby poussin to the poularde and capon.

Poussin: the smallest variety used for roasting. One poussin makes a portion, the weight being 300-450g (10-16oz).

Poularde de grain (Spring Chicken): used for roasting and grilling, these are usually under 10 weeks old and weigh from 600-900g (1½-2lbs).

Poule: the mature hen chicken (over ten months old) weighing up to 2¼kg (5lbs). Used mainly for chicken soup.

Poularde: these are specially bred hens weighing up to 3kg (6½lbs), used for roasting, pot roasting and shallow frying.

Suprême de volaille
à la mangue
Breast of chicken stuffed with mango

Ingredients (for 4 people)

4		poularde breasts (150g (5oz) each) without skin salt, freshly ground pepper
120g	(4¼oz)	mangoes, cut into cubes
5g	(¼oz)	flour
2		eggs
50g	(2oz)	coconut flakes } mixed
50g	(2oz)	white breadcrumbs } together
50g	(2oz)	clarified butter
200g	(7oz)	turned courgettes
20g	(¾oz)	butter
200g	(7oz)	turned carrots (glazed, see page 40) a little sugar for glazing the carrots

Method

- Cut the well trimmed chicken breasts lengthwise.
- Lightly bat the breasts, without fillets, and season with salt and pepper.
- Stuff with the cubes of mango and lay the fillets on top.
- Lightly dust the breasts with flour.
- Coat with beaten egg and the coconut flakes mixed with the breadcrumbs.
- Sauté carefully until golden brown in the clarified butter, which should not be too hot.
- Blanch and sauté the seasoned courgettes in butter and mix with the glazed carrots.
- Arrange on a suitable dish and place the fried chicken breasts on top.
- Sprinkle with the remaining brown butter and serve immediately.

Blanc de volaille sous cloche

Breast of chicken with mushroom sauce

Ingredients (for 4 people)

4		poularde breasts (160g (5½oz) each) salt, freshly ground pepper
40g	(1½oz)	butter
10cl	(4fl oz)	white wine
30cl	(½ pint)	double cream
50g	(2oz)	butter, to finish
30cl	(½ pint)	poultry stock (see recipe 1)
200g	(7oz)	small raw mushrooms

Method

- Remove the skin from the chicken breasts and clean the wing bones with a knife.
- Season the chicken breasts with salt and pepper. Sweat in butter without giving them any colour.
- Remove the butter, add the white wine and allow to reduce.
- Add the poultry stock and mushrooms.
- Bring to boil, cover and poach until tender.
- Remove the chicken breast and keep warm.
- Add cream and reduce to the required consistency.
- Strain through a muslin and monté carefully with butter.
- Season with salt and pepper.
- Arrange the breasts on warm glass plates, pour over the sauce and cover with glass lids.

Suprême de volaille Paul Bocuse

Breast of chicken in puff pastry

This dish is created for Paul Bocuse, whom I consider to be among the greatest chefs in the world. His culinary influence has spread throughout the world, and I treasure the experience of having worked with him. His kitchen is run with the precision of a watch, producing dishes of superb quality. Paul Bocuse is known for his eagerness, and has been nicknamed 'the motivator of men'. Thank you Paul for what you have done for our profession.

Ingredients (for 4 people)

4		pieces of chicken breast (130g (4¾oz) each)
		salt, freshly ground pepper
20g	(¾oz)	butter
60g	(2½oz)	finely chopped raw mushroom
60g	(2½oz)	chicken mousseline (see recipe 15)
4		thin pancakes (halved) (see recipe 178)
200g	(7oz)	puff pastry (see recipe 19)
1		egg yolk
15cl	(¼ pint)	truffle sauce (see recipe 27)

Method

- Season the chicken breasts and sauté in butter without browning them.
- Mix the chopped mushroom with the chicken mousseline and season with salt and pepper.
- Place the mixture on the cooled chicken breasts.
- Cover the chicken breasts with pancake halves and roll them attractively in the puff pastry. Brush with egg yolk, allow to stand for 30 minutes then bake in a moderate oven at 200°C (400°F) for 12-15 minutes.
- Serve the truffle sauce separately. ▶

Note It is important that the wing bone of the chicken is also packed into the puff pastry. It is also important to see that the pancakes are placed in such a way that the suprême does not come into contact with the pastry, otherwise it will be very difficult to bake the pastry right through.

Suprême de pintadeaux aux olives noires et vertes
Breast of guinea fowl with black and green olives

Ingredients (for 4 people)

2		guinea fowl, 1.2kg (2½lb) each
		salt, freshly ground pepper
2cl		olive oil
20g	(¾fl oz)	butter
5cl	(2fl oz)	Madeira

Method
- Pluck, singe and draw the guinea fowl.
- Separate the breasts carefully.
- Saw off the wing bones with great care.
- The legs of the guinea fowl can be roasted or poached and used elsewhere.
- Make a stock from the carcasses (see recipe 10).
- Lightly bat the guinea fowl breasts and season with salt and pepper.
- Sauté until juicy in the olive oil and butter in a suitable sautoir.
- Remove the breasts and keep warm.
- Pour off the fat.
- Add the Madeira, allow to reduce a little and add to the sauce (see below).
- Arrange the guinea fowl breasts, cover with the well seasoned sauce and serve immediately. ▶

PLATE 15
Màgret de canard grillé-Nossi-Bé. (Grilled duck's breast with green pepper-corns) Recipe 153.

Recipes 145 & 146

Sauce

10g	(½oz)	finely chopped shallot
10g	(½oz)	butter
5cl	(2fl oz)	white wine
40g	(1½oz)	tomates concassées (see recipe 36)
20cl	(6fl oz)	guinea fowl stock (see above)
20cl	(6fl oz)	Madeira sauce (see recipe 30)
8		black olives
8		green olives
		both with stones removed
		and cut into cubes of ½cm (¼in)
8		tarragon leaves, coarsely chopped
40g	(1½oz)	butter, to finish
		salt, freshly ground pepper

Method

- Sweat the finely chopped shallot in butter, without letting it colour.
- Add the white wine and bring to the boil.
- Add the tomates concassées and poultry stock and reduce to half its original volume.
- Add the Madeira sauce and cook until a lightly flowing sauce is produced.
- Mix in the olives and tarragon.
- Carefully monté with butter.
- Season with salt and pepper.
- Arrange the hot sauce on a warm plate with the guinea fowl on top and serve immediately.

PLATE 16
Poussin aux légumes grillés. (Grilled baby chicken with grilled vegetables) Recipe 149.

Recipe 146

Délice de volaille farci à la banane

Breast of chicken with banana

Ingredients (for 4 people)

4		pieces of chicken breast (each about 100g (4oz)) without skin or bones
		salt, freshly ground pepper
		a few drops of Angostura bitters
4		slices of ham, thinly cut
5g	(¼oz)	butter
4		small bananas
		some flour
		egg ⎫
		white breadcrumbs ⎬ for coating
100g	(4oz)	⎭
50g	(2oz)	butter
20cl	(6fl oz)	curry sauce (see recipe 32)

Method

- Flatten the chicken breasts, season with salt, pepper and Angostura bitters.
- Sauté the slices of ham quickly in butter and lay them on the chicken.
- Cut the bananas neatly (lengthwise if necessary), lay them on the ham and carefully roll it all up together.
- Coat with flour, egg and breadcrumbs.
- Sauté until golden brown in the butter, which should not be too hot.
- Serve the curry sauce separately.

Note I would recommend serving the chicken breasts, either whole or in slices, on pilaff rice.

Coquelet à la vapeur
Steamed baby chicken with carrot leaf sauce

Ingredients (for 4 people)

4		baby chickens
200g	(7oz)	sweetbreads
160g	(5½oz)	chicken meat
50g	(2oz)	chopped onions
20g	(¾oz)	butter
120g	(4½oz)	mushrooms, diced
50g	(2oz)	morels
		salt, freshly ground pepper
10cl	(4fl oz)	Port
40cl	(¾ pint)	chicken stock (see recipe 1)
30g	(1¼oz)	carrots, cut into strips
40g	(1½oz)	asparagus tips
30g	(1¼oz)	haricot beans, blanched
10g	(½oz)	button onions, blanched
5g	(¼oz)	fresh morels, for garnish

Method

- Singe, draw and clean the baby chickens.
- Remove the skin from the sweetbreads and chicken meat and trim.
- Sweat the onions in butter, add the mushrooms, morels, sweetbreads and chicken meat and season.
- Add the Port and chicken stock and simmer slowly.
- Remove the sweetbreads, chicken meat, mushrooms and morels from the stock, allow to cool and cut into small cubes.
- Greatly reduce the stock, mix the finely chopped sweetbreads, chicken meat, mushrooms and morels together well, add to the stock, season and stuff the poussins with the mixture.
- Wrap the baby chickens in aluminium foil and cook over steam for about 20 minutes.

▶

Recipe 148

- Just before the end of the cooking time, add the vegetables and steam keeping them *al dente*.
- Arrange the chickens on the sauce in a suitable dish and garnish with the vegetables.

Sauce

10g	(½oz)	carrot
10g	(½oz)	courgette
10g	(½oz)	mushrooms
30cl	(½ pint)	chicken stock (see recipe 1)
100g	(4oz)	tops of carrot leaves
20g	(¾oz)	soft cheese
10cl	(4fl oz)	double cream
		salt, freshly ground pepper
		lemon juice

} cut into strips

Method

- Wash the vegetables and cook them in the chicken stock.
- Allow to cool a little and liquidise.
- Heat up again and if necessary thin the mixture down with a little chicken stock.
- Remove the stalks from the carrot leaves, wash, blanch, liquidise and add to the sauce.
- Finish this vegetable sauce with the soft cheese and cream.
- Season well with salt, pepper and a little lemon juice.

‘To produce good food, you must be a happy person.’

Poussin aux légumes grillés
Grilled baby chicken with grilled vegetables

Ingredients (for 4 people)

4		baby chickens
20cl	(6fl oz)	olive oil
220g	(8oz)	new potatoes, peeled and sliced
200g	(7oz)	broccoli, cleaned and cut into pieces
100g	(4oz)	young small carrots, peeled without the green tops cut away
120g	(4½oz)	small courgettes
100g	(4oz)	young tender leek, cut into pieces approximately 6cm (2¼in) long
20g	(¾oz)	tomato coulis (see Glossary) salt, freshly ground pepper

Method (See Plate 16)

- Draw and singe the baby chickens, cut them down the back, press them flat and remove the ribs and legs. Season them with salt and freshly ground pepper.
- Marinate the baby chickens and the prepared vegetables separately in olive oil for about 30 minutes.
- Grill the chicken and vegetables separately at a moderate heat.
- Arrange the chickens and garnish attractively with the crispy grilled vegetables.
- Serve the tomato coulis separately.

Note The grilled vegetables can be seasoned with salt just before service. The chicken legs are not served in this recipe. They can be used in a mousseline or in another dish.

Pollo alla Romana
Chicken with mixed peppers

Ingredients (for 4 people)

2		chickens (1.1kg (2¼lb) each)
40g	(1½oz)	melted chicken fat
50g	(2oz)	onions, cut into slices
1		clove of garlic, finely chopped
100g	(4oz)	fresh mushrooms
100g	(4oz)	red peppers
100g	(4oz)	green peppers } cut into quarters
100g	(4oz)	yellow peppers
200g	(7oz)	tomatoes, diced
20cl	(6fl oz)	white wine
60cl	(1 pint)	brown poultry stock (see recipe 3)
		some fresh thyme, marjoram and rosemary
4		basil leaves
		chopped parsley
		salt, freshly ground pepper

Method

- The chicken should be drawn and singed and divided into 8 pieces.
- Sauté the chicken pieces in chicken fat.
- Add the onions, garlic, mushrooms and peppers and mix in well.
- Add the tomatoes, white wine and poultry stock and bring to the boil.
- Add the fresh herbs and basil leaves, cover and cook in a medium oven for 10 minutes.
- Remove the chicken pieces and vegetables, reduce the sauce to the required consistency, then adjust seasoning.
- Arrange the chicken pieces and vegetables on a suitable dish. ▶

- Cover with the sauce, sprinkle with parsley and serve.

Note To ensure that this dish has a good colour, it is important not to overcook the peppers.

Poularde sautée aux écrevisses
Sautéd chicken with crayfish

Ingredients (for 4 people)

1		chicken (about 2.2kg (4½lb))
		salt, freshly ground pepper
40g	(1½oz)	melted poultry fat
40g	(1½oz)	mirepoix
20cl	(6fl oz)	white wine
40cl	(¾ pint)	brown poultry stock (see recipe 3)
20cl	(6fl oz)	cream
20cl	(6fl oz)	crayfish sauce (see recipe 24)
50g	(2oz)	butter, to finish
3cl		Cognac
10g	(½oz)	morels, carefully washed
5g	(¼oz)	butter, to sauté the morels
8		crayfish (with tail flesh removed)

Method
- Draw the chicken, singe and divide into 8 pieces.
- Sauté the seasoned chicken in the poultry fat, without browning it. Add the mirepoix and sauté for 5 more minutes very carefully.
- Pour off the fat.
- Add the white wine and reduce, add the poultry stock, cover and cook in the oven for 12-15 minutes.

▶

- Remove the chicken and reduce the stock to half its original volume.
- Add the cream and crayfish sauce and reduce to the required consistency.
- Strain the sauce, and monté with the soft butter.
- Flavour with Cognac, salt and pepper.
- Arrange the chicken in a suitable dish and cover with the sauce.
- Sauté the morels in butter.
- Garnish with the pre-heated crayfish tails, the sautéd morels and 8 crayfish.

Fricassée de volaille au vinaigre
Chicken fricassée with vinegar sauce

Ingredients (for 4 people)

1		chicken (2.2kg (4½lb))
		salt, freshly ground pepper
40g	(1½oz)	melted chicken fat
50g	(2oz)	finely chopped shallots
15cl	(¼ pint)	white wine vinegar
10cl	(4fl oz)	white wine
30cl	(½ pint)	white poultry stock (see recipe 1)
		a little meat glaze (see recipe 9)
100g	(4oz)	tomatoes, diced
40g	(1½oz)	butter, to finish
		a little chopped parsley

Method
- The chicken should be drawn, singed and then divided into 8 pieces.
- Season them with salt and pepper and sweat in chicken fat without browning it.
- Remove the fat, add the shallots and continue to sweat.

▶

- First add the vinegar, then the white wine. Reduce a little then add the poultry stock.
- Add the meat glaze, cover and cook in the oven for about 10-15 minutes.
- Remove the pieces of chicken and keep warm, reduce the liquid to half its original volume, strain, then add the diced tomatoes.
- Work in the butter gradually and season with salt and pepper.
- Arrange the chicken pieces in a suitable dish and cover with the sauce. Garnish with chopped parsley.

Màgret de canard grillé — Nossi-Bé

Grilled duck's breast with green peppercorns

Nossi-Bé is a mountain in Madagascar, the island famous for its peppers.

Ingredients (for 4 people)

2		ducks (approximately 2.5kg (5lb))
		salt, freshly ground pepper
2cl	(¾fl oz)	peanut oil
20g	(¾oz)	butter
30g	(1¼oz)	unrefined sugar
2		apples (100g (4oz) net)
5cl	(2fl oz)	white wine
20g	(¾oz)	green peppercorns
20cl	(6fl oz)	brown duck stock (see recipe 12)

Method (See Plate 15)
- Pluck the ducks clean, singe and draw them.
- Cut off the neck and head, remove the legs carefully and keep for use in another dish. ▶

- Cut out the collar bone and back bone and chop into small pieces (these with the neck can be used to make a brown duck stock).
- Cut the flattened double breast in two, so that you have 2 pieces of breast.
- Remove skin and bones, season, lightly coat with oil and cook under a hot grill.
- Meanwhile mix the butter and sugar into a light caramel.
- Peel and cut each apple into 8 pieces, and add to the caramel.
- Add the white wine and allow to simmer for 2-3 minutes.
- Arrange the underdone duck breasts on a plate and garnish with the glazed apples and green peppercorns.
- Serve the duck stock separately.

Note To prevent the duck breasts from drying out, it is important that they are served slightly rare.

Chapter 10

Game Dishes

Game Dishes

Game is the term used for the meat of wild animals. Deer, hare, stag are the most common ground game, the meat of which is considered equal to that of any other animal. It is tender and is easily digestible. Its nutritional value is also equal to that of other meat. It reaches its highest standard in autumn, that is during the hunting season.

Feathered game is included among those animals which are hunted and therefore may not be shot during the close season which is laid down by law. Feathered game includes wild fowl, pheasant, partridge, white grouse, grouse, wild duck and other fowl. The meat of feathered game is less rich in fat than that of domestic poultry and is generally easy to digest. Compared with the meat of domestic poultry it has a deeper and stronger taste. Young birds have soft breast bones, a beak which is not too hard and down under the feathers. Young partridges must have yellow feet.

The best time for eating pheasant, the most popular game bird, is from October until the beginning of February. Pheasant must be carefully roasted. If it is cooked at too high a temperature or for too long, it will become dry. To prevent this happening, it should be barded, i.e. the breast should be covered with a thin slice of bacon. Pheasant should be prepared while fresh or just briefly hung for a couple of days — hanging for weeks until it is overripe is no longer recommended.

Prime quality hares are young — about 4-8 months and their meat is not as dark as that of older animals which is dark red. Young hares are very tender, the meat of old animals tends to be dry. Hare can be kept by hanging unskinned by the feet.

Venison is usually very lean meat. Animals under about 3 years have tender and easily digestible meat but older animals are tougher.

Mignons de chevreuil à la purée de persil
Mignons of venison with parsley purée

Ingredients (for 4 people)

12		mignons of venison (40g (1½oz) each)
		salt, freshly ground pepper
20g	(¾oz)	butter
20cl	(6fl oz)	red wine (Burgundy)
40cl	(¾ pint)	game stock (see recipe 10)
50g	(2oz)	butter, to finish
20cl	(6fl oz)	beef blood
400g	(14oz)	small chanterelles
3g		finely chopped shallot

Method

- Season the well trimmed mignons on both sides.
- Sauté them pink in the butter and keep hot.
- Remove the butter, add the red wine and reduce.
- Add the game stock, allow to reduce a little, add the butter and beef blood, working in a little at a time, strain and season with salt and pepper. Do not boil.
- Clean the chanterelles well and sauté in butter with the chopped shallot and season with salt and pepper.
- Place the well seasoned sauce on a suitable dish and arrange the mignons on it.
- Garnish with the chanterelles.
- Serve the parsley purée separately.

Parsley purée

250g	(9oz)	parsley without stalks
5cl	(2fl oz)	double cream

- Wash the parsley well and steam with a little water and butter.
- Liquidise without water.
- Finish off purée with the cream and season with salt and pepper.

Médaillons de chevreuil belle forestière
Sautéd medallions of venison with mushrooms in game sauce

Ingredients (for 4 people)

8		medallions of venison (70g (2¾oz) each)
		salt, freshly ground pepper
40g	(1½oz)	butter
10g	(½oz)	finely chopped shallot
100g	(4oz)	small mushrooms
50g	(2oz)	yellow boletus (cèpes), sliced
50g	(2oz)	small chanterelles
50g	(2oz)	small morels
5cl	(2fl oz)	Cognac
10cl	(4fl oz)	Madeira
30cl	(½ pint)	game stock (see recipe 10)
20cl	(6fl oz)	double cream
		a little chopped parsley

Method

- Season the well trimmed medallions and fry in the butter until pink.
- Remove the butter, add the chopped shallot and sweat for a short while.
- Add the mushrooms, chanterelles, cèpes and morels and sweat for 3 to 4 minutes. Season.
- Flame with the Cognac and Madeira and add the game stock.
- Allow to reduce a little and add the cream.
- Bring to the boil and season with salt and pepper.
- Arrange the medallions, cover with the sauce and garnish with parsley.

Râble de lièvre rôti au sang
Roast saddle of hare with game sauce

Ingredients (for 4 people)

2		saddle of hare, medium size
40g	(1½oz)	butter
		salt, freshly ground pepper

Marinade

20g	(¾oz)	finely cut carrot
10g	(½oz)	finely chopped shallot
80g	(3¼oz)	finely cut celery
2		juniper berries
2		cloves
½		bay leaf
		some thyme
		salt, freshly ground pepper
5cl	(2fl oz)	red wine

Method

- Remove the sinews and nerves from the saddle with a knife.
- Place the well trimmed saddle in a deep bowl.
- Make a marinade with the carrots, shallots, celery, spices, seasoning and red wine and pour over the saddle.
- Marinate for 12 hours covered with greaseproof paper.
- Remove the saddle, season lightly with salt and pepper.
- Heat the butter in a suitable pan, put in the hare and carefully roast on both sides for about 10 to 12 minutes in a hot oven, until pink.
- Remove the hare and keep warm.
- Pour off the butter from the pan and add to the marinade.
- Allow to boil and reduce and then strain.
- Add this stock to the game sauce (see recipe 29). ▶

Recipe 156

- Arrange the hare on a suitable serving dish, cover with the well seasoned sauce and serve immediately.
- Serve the rest of the sauce separately.

Suprême de faisan aux amandes
Breast of pheasant with almonds

Ingredients (for 4 people)

2		young pheasants
		salt, freshly ground pepper
120g	(4½oz)	unsalted bacon (or barding lard)
40g	(1½oz)	butter
5cl	(2fl oz)	dry Sherry
50g	(2oz)	shredded almonds, not roasted

Method

- Remove the pheasant breasts carefully from the carcass.
- Season with salt and pepper.
- Wrap each breast separately in the thinly sliced bacon or lard and bind with fine string.
- Melt half the butter in a pan.
- Add the pheasants' breasts and roast in a hot oven for about 5-6 minutes, basting constantly.
- Remove the breasts and keep warm.
- Pour away the fat and add the Sherry to the cooking juices.
- Bring to the boil and add to the sauce (see below).
- Remove the barding lard from the breasts.
- Cut the meat carefully into thin even strips (aiguillettes).
- Arrange on a suitable dish.

▶

- Sauté the shredded almonds carefully in the remaining butter until golden brown then sprinkle them evenly over the meat.
- Serve the delicately seasoned sauce (see below) separately.

1

Sauce

		carcasses of the pheasants
2cl	(¾fl oz)	peanut oil
10g	(½oz)	shallot ⎫ cut in
30g	(1¼oz)	celery ⎬ small
30g	(1¼oz)	carrot ⎭ cubes
½		bay leaf
½		sprig of thyme
15cl	(¼ pint)	white wine
20cl	(6fl oz)	game stock (see recipe 10)
30g	(1¼oz)	butter, to finish
		salt, freshly ground pepper

Method
- Chop the carcasses, legs and necks of the pheasants into small pieces.
- Sauté well on all sides in hot oil.
- Add the shallot, celery, carrot and herbs, and cook slowly in the oven to flavour the sauce, checking occasionally.
- Pour off the fat and add the white wine.
- Add the stock and allow to simmer for about 30 minutes.
- Strain the stock and reduce to the required consistency.
- At the end, monté with butter and season with salt and pepper.

0

Grouse rôti à l'écossaise
Roast Scottish grouse

Ingredients (for 4 people)

4		Scottish grouse (450g (1lb))
		salt, freshly ground pepper
80g	(3¼oz)	barding lard, cut into thin slices
10cl	(4fl oz)	peanut oil
100g	(4oz)	fine mirepoix (see page 297)
20cl	(6fl oz)	red wine
40cl	(¾ pint)	game stock (see recipe 10)
4		heart-shaped bread croûtons with farce à gratin (see recipe 16)
40g	(1½oz)	browned breadcrumbs
		a little watercress
4 portions		potato gaufrettes
10cl	(4fl oz)	bread sauce (see recipe 159)

Method
- The grouse should be plucked, flamed, drawn and bound.
- Season the grouse and cover with the barding lard.
- Heat the oil in a suitable pan, roast the grouse on both sides, lay them on their backs and roast with the mirepoix in the oven for 7-8 minutes at a good heat until pink, basting all the time.
- Keep the grouse warm.
- Pour off the fat, add the red wine to the cooking juices and reduce.
- Add the game stock and reduce to the required consistency, season with salt and pepper and strain.
- Remove the barding lard from the grouse and give them a little more colour in the oven.
- Arrange the grouse on the croûtons with farce à gratin.
- Garnish with watercress, brown breadcrumbs and pommes gaufrettes (lattice french fried potatoes). Serve with bread sauce.

▶

Note The slices of white bread can be fried in butter or toasted under the grill. The brown breadcrumbs are served to soak up the blood and juices from the grouse.

Bread sauce
(For the grouse)

Ingredients

15cl	(¼ pint)	milk
1		small onion peeled and pickled with clove and a small bay leaf
		salt
25g	(1oz)	white breadcrumbs
2cl	(¾fl oz)	cream
10g	(½oz)	butter

Method

- Bring the milk with the onion, clove, bay leaf and salt to the boil.
- Add the white breadcrumbs and allow to simmer for 10 minutes.
- Remove the onion, bay leaf and clove.
- Add the cream and butter and whisk until smooth.
- Season with salt.

‘Remember, bad cooking means not only expensive buying, but waste in cooking, bad health, bad temper, and starved good natures.’

Recipes 158 & 159

Duo de cailles farcies au riz sauvage
Stuffed quails with wild rice

Ingredients (for 4 people)

8		quails
		salt, freshly ground pepper
1 small		crépine (caul fat) soaked, to wrap the quails in
40g	(1½oz)	butter
20g	(¾oz)	finely chopped carrot
5g	(¼oz)	finely chopped shallot
20g	(¾oz)	finely chopped celery
8		juniper berries
5cl	(2fl oz)	Madeira
20cl	(6fl oz)	brown poultry stock (see recipe 3)
5cl	(2fl oz)	meat glaze (see recipe 9)

Method

- Cut the quails down the back with a sharp knife and remove the bones.
- Remove the liver and heart and set aside.
- Remove the breast bones and pull out the upper thigh bone.
- Season the quails with salt and freshly ground pepper and stuff with the well seasoned wild rice mixture (see below).
- Return the quails to their original shape and bind with a small piece of string.
- Pack the quails individually in the crépine.
- Season with salt and pepper.
- Heat the butter in a suitable pan, put in the stuffed quails and fry on both sides.
- Add the chopped shallot, carrot, celery and the juniper berries and roast until crisp in a moderately hot oven for 15 to 20 minutes, basting constantly.

►

- Remove the quails and keep warm.
- Discard the butter and add the Madeira to the cooking juices.
- Add the brown poultry stock and reduce to half the original volume.
- Add the meat glaze, bring to the boil and strain.
- Season with salt and pepper.
- Remove the quails from the crépine, arrange them on a suitable dish, and cover with the sauce.

Stuffing

5g	(¼oz)	finely chopped shallot
10g	(½oz)	butter
		liver and heart of the quails cut into small cubes
		salt, freshly ground pepper
120g	(4½oz)	cooked wild rice
20g	(¾oz)	apple cut into small cubes
4cl	(1½fl oz)	double cream
1		egg yolk
		a little thyme

Method

- Sweat the chopped shallot in the butter.
- Season the pieces of heart and liver, sauté them and then keep cool.
- Mix the pieces of liver with the cooked wild rice and the pieces of apple.
- Add the cream and bind with the egg yolk.
- Season with thyme, salt and pepper.

Wild rice

This needs to cook for 40-45 minutes in plenty of boiling salted water.

Perdreau rôti aux raisins de muscat
Partridge with grapes in pastry

Ingredients (for 4 people)

4		young partridges
		salt, freshly ground pepper
40g	(1½oz)	butter
3cl	(1fl oz)	Sherry
5cl	(2fl oz)	game stock (see recipe 10)
200g	(7oz)	white muscatel grapes, peeled and stoned
150g	(5oz)	puff pastry (see recipe 19)

Method

- Pluck, singe, draw and bind the partridges.
- Season inside and out with salt and pepper.
- Heat the butter in a cocotte and gently sauté the partridges on both sides until brown.
- Remove the partridges from the cocotte and take off the string.
- Discard the butter, add the Sherry to the cooking juices.
- Add the game stock and muscatel grapes.
- Put in the partridges.
- Season the stock with salt and pepper and cover with a lid.
- Seal the edges of the lid with puff pastry and bake in a hot oven for 7-8 minutes so that when they are being served, they remain pink.
- Serve in the cocotte.

Note The partridges should be roasted rare. It is a good idea to open the cocotte in front of the guests, so that none of the taste of the partridge is lost.

Aiguillettes de canard sauvage Albert Schnell
Fillets of wild duck with juniper berry sauce

Albert Schnell is the Executive Chef of the Queen Elizabeth Hotel, Montreal. I spent three happy and productive years working with him. He is, in my opinion, one of the greatest chefs in the world — but he is more than that. He is also a wonderful person.

Ingredients (for 4 people)

2		young wild ducks
		salt, freshly ground pepper
3cl	(1fl oz)	peanut oil
10cl	(4fl oz)	red wine

Method
- Pluck, singe and carefully draw the wild duck.
- Season inside and out with salt and pepper and, in the heated peanut oil, roast in a suitable pan in a hot oven for 12-13 minutes, until pink, basting constantly.
- Remove from the pan and keep warm.
- Pour off the cooking fat from the pan, add the red wine and reduce to half its original volume.
- Use this stock for the sauce (see below).
- Separate the legs of the wild duck and use elsewhere.
- Pull off the skin from the breast and cut the breast lengthwise into ½cm (¼in) thick pieces.
- Pour the well seasoned sauce on to a suitable dish, lay the slices of wild duck, lightly seasoned with salt and pepper, on top and serve immediately.

Juniper berry sauce

10cl	(4fl oz)	Madeira
30cl	(½ pint)	red wine (Burgundy)
5		juniper berries

▶

		some thyme and bay leaves
50cl	(18fl oz)	wild duck stock (see recipe 12)
10cl	(4fl oz)	veal blood
2cl	(¾fl oz)	single cream
		salt, freshly ground pepper
40g	(1½oz)	butter, to finish

Method

- Almost completely reduce the Madeira and red wine with the juniper berries, thyme and bay leaves.
- Add the wild duck stock and reduce to half its original volume.
- Mix the veal blood with the cream and gradually add to the sauce.
- Strain through a fine sieve.
- Carefully monté with butter and season with salt and pepper.

Chapter 11

Vegetables

Vegetables

Vegetables play a particularly large part in the preparation and presentation of various dishes. There are innumerable different types of vegetables, many different ways of cooking them and an almost inexhaustible variety of taste. They complement small and large dishes and they perfectly complete a menu. Moreover, vegetables are particularly valuable for their content of minerals, vitamins, extracts and essential oils. In addition they supply bulk material (cellulose) which is of great importance to metabolism. When carefully prepared, vegetables have the ability to absorb fat, protein, sugar and seasoning. Since the components which are of nutritional-physiological value are very sensitive, vegetables must be treated and prepared with great care. Fresh vegetables should be used immediately.

Here are the rules for cooking green beans, peas, spinach and asparagus. Heat a saucepan containing plenty of water and 10g (½oz) of salt per litre (1¾ pints); do not cover. As soon as the water is boiling add the vegetables and allow to boil vigorously all the time. As soon as the vegetables are just cooked, remove quickly, season and, for best results, serve immediately, or finish preparing according to taste, for example, toss in butter. If the vegetables cannot be used immediately, it is advisable to place them in their own boiling water or vegetable stock water on ice. The advantage of this is that the vegetables retain their taste instead of losing it under running water.

It must be remembered that the vegetables should remain slightly crisp; cooking them for too long will adversely affect their flavour, colour and shape and the proteins will become hard or tough which renders the digestive process difficult or imposible. Various vitamins and flavours will be partly or completely destroyed. Chlorophyll and other natural colours will

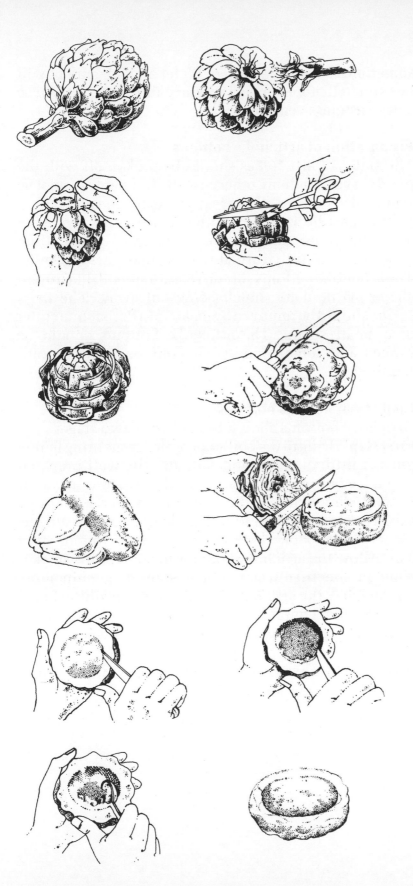

Stages in the
preparation of
artichoke bottoms, as
described on page 256.

sometimes be greatly altered. Water and fat content will be extracted more than is necessary and the result will be a dry, tasteless vegetable.

Preparation of artichoke bottoms

The stalks of artichokes should be broken off with the hand (never cut them, otherwise the filaments cannot be removed). Remove all the leaves one by one and cut off the top part horizontally with a sharp knife, removing about three quarters of the whole. The green of the bottom should be carefully turned with a small turning knife. The artichoke bottoms should retain a smooth half round shape, without too much being cut away. The hairs inside should be removed by means of a Parisienne cutter or a small spoon. The artichoke bottoms should be rubbed with lemon and kept in cold lemon water until required.

Cooking artichoke bottoms

Artichoke bottoms should be cooked in two stages:

First step Bring to the boil some water containing lemon juice, a little olive oil and salt, add the well prepared artichoke bottoms and blanch for three to four minutes.

Second step Bring to the boil some water containing salt, veal kidney fat and a little lemon juice. Add the blanched artichoke bottoms, cover and simmer until soft. Allow the artichoke bottoms to cool in this stock.

Note In the first water which should contain more lemon juice, the artichoke bottoms remain white. In the second water containing less lemon juice, the artichoke bottoms keep their white colour but improve in taste. If the artichoke bottoms are not to be used immediately, they should always be allowed to cool in the stock, otherwise they will lose colour and taste.

Pommes Maison
Potatoes home-style

Ingredients (for 4 people)

400g	(14oz)	potatoes
30g	(1¼oz)	melted chicken fat
30g	(1¼oz)	butter
		salt, freshly ground pepper

Method

- Peel the potatoes and wash thoroughly, cut into thin strips and dry them well.
- Heat the chicken fat and butter in a suitable sauteuse.
- Season the potato strips with salt and pepper and add to the pan.
- Sauté them until light brown in colour.
- Form the potatoes into the shape of a cake with the help of a spatula and sauté on both sides until golden brown.
- Arrange on a flat dish.

Note The potatoes may be cut on a mandoline (a vegetable slicer).

Pommes à l'ail gratinées
Gratin of potatoes with cream and garlic

Ingredients (for 4 people)

600g	(1¼lb)	potatoes (longish in shape, approximately 2cm (¾in) in diameter)

		salt, nutmeg, freshly ground pepper
1		small garlic clove
30cl	(½ pint)	double cream
100g	(4oz)	finely grated cheese
		(well ripened Emmental or Gruyère)
15g	(½oz)	butter

Method

- Peel the potatoes just before they are needed.
- Cut the potatoes into 2mm (⅛in) thick slices.
- Place them on a cloth to dry and season with salt, nutmeg and pepper.
- Rub a gratin dish with the peeled garlic clove.
- Add the seasoned potatoes and arrange in a nice pattern on top.
- Cover the dish and cook in a bain-marie in the oven for about 1 hour.
- Fifteen minutes before serving sprinkle with the grated cheese, dot with butter and brown under the grill.

Note The potato gratin should be golden brown on top but not dry. This goes particularly well with lamb dishes.

Lentilles braisées
Braised lentils

Ingredients (for 4 people)

250g	(9oz)	lentils
60g	(2½oz)	smoked bacon, cut in pieces
100g	(4oz)	onions
40g	(1½oz)	carrot } finely cut
30g	(1¼oz)	leek
100g	(4oz)	potatoes, cut into small dice
40g	(1½oz)	tomato purée

▶

60cl	(1 pint)	brown veal stock (see recipe 4)
		salt, freshly ground pepper
1		small clove of garlic
1cl	(½fl oz)	wine vinegar
1		sardine fillet

Method

- Soak the lentils in cold water for 2-3 hours.
- Sauté the pieces of bacon.
- Add the vegetables and tomato purée, continue to sauté and then add the veal stock and garlic.
- Add the soaked lentils (without the water) and bring to the boil.
- Season with salt and pepper, skim and cook until just done.
- Remove the garlic.
- Purée a quarter of the cooked lentils in a liquidiser and bind the rest of the lentils with this.
- Finally add the finely chopped sardine fillet and vinegar and season with salt and pepper.

Note Lentilles braisées are a good accompaniment for lamb dishes.

Trianon de légumes
Three selected vegetables

Ingredients (for 4 people)

300g	(10oz)	medium sized courgettes
200g	(7oz)	small aubergines of similar shape
		salt, freshly ground white pepper
300g	(10oz)	small tomatoes
30g	(1¼oz)	butter
		a few thyme leaves
40g	(1½oz)	white breadcrumbs, toasted
2cl	(¾fl oz)	olive oil

▶

Method
- Wash the courgettes well and cut off the ends.
- Peel with a knife in the usual way and cut into slices 2mm (⅛in) thick.
- Prepare the aubergines in exactly the same way.
- Season the courgettes and aubergines with salt and pepper.
- Meanwhile blanch and peel the tomatoes and cut into slices.
- Heat the butter, then sauté the courgettes and aubergines in it.
- Grease a gratin dish with the remaining butter.
- Arrange layers of courgettes, aubergines and seasoned tomatoes in the dish.
- Sprinkle with thyme leaves.
- Arrange the toasted breadcrumbs on the top.
- Sprinkle with olive oil and cook in medium hot oven for 12-15 minutes.

Note This dish goes well with a cold meal (but do not store in the refrigerator). It can be served cold.

Crêpes de maïs
Pancakes with creamed sweetcorn

Ingredients (for 4 people)

300g	(10oz)	corn on the cob
15cl	(¼ pint)	milk
10cl	(4fl oz)	double cream
1		egg
1		egg yolk
60g	(2½oz)	flour
		salt, a little nutmeg, freshly ground pepper
20g	(¾oz)	butter, to fry pancakes

▶

Method

- Wash the corn on the cob well and blanch in the milk.
- Remove the corn on the cob and chop roughly (keep the milk for the batter).
- Mix together the milk, cream, egg, egg yolk and flour.
- Add the roughly chopped corn on the cob and flavour with salt, nutmeg and pepper.
- Warm the butter gently in a pan, measure out small pancakes with a spoon and fry golden brown on both sides.

Note These small pancakes make a very good accompaniment to grilled and roasted meat, and also to poultry.

Purée d'artichauts
Purée of artichokes

Ingredients (for 4 people)

350g	(12oz)	cooked artichoke bottoms (see page 256)
15cl	(¼ pint)	double cream
30g	(1¼oz)	butter
		a little sugar
		salt, freshly ground white pepper

Method

- Strain the artichoke bottoms finely and then press through a fine sieve.
- Reduce the double cream to half its original volume.
- Add the artichoke purée.
- Finish with the butter.
- Season with a little sugar, salt and pepper.

Note This fine, delicate purée goes particularly well with lamb dishes.

Mousseline de betterave
Mousseline of beetroot

Ingredients (for 4 people)

250g	(9oz)	uncooked beetroot
20g	(¾oz)	butter
15cl	(¼ pint)	double cream
1		egg, separated
		salt, freshly ground white pepper

Method

- Peel the beetroots and cut into thin slices.
- Sweat in butter, add the cream, cover and cook until soft.
- Leave to cool for a while and then mix in the egg yolk.
- Pass through a fine sieve, add the lightly whipped egg white and season.
- Put the mixture into small buttered moulds and poach in a bain-marie in a medium hot oven for about 35-40 minutes.

Note Smooth over the top of the vegetable purée when it is in the moulds so that it will stand straight on the plate when it is turned out. Place a piece of paper on the bottom of the bain-marie so that, during poaching, the moulds do not move or knock together. During poaching in the bain-marie, make sure that the moulds are standing three-quarters deep in water and the water should be kept just below boiling point, otherwise the purée will become perforated. Before turning out allow to stand for 4-5 minutes so that the mixture slides out of the mould more easily.

Mousseline de choux de Bruxelles
Mousseline of Brussels sprouts

Ingredients (for 4 people)
300g	(10oz)	Brussels sprouts
10cl	(4fl oz)	double cream
40g	(1½oz)	butter
		salt, freshly ground white pepper

Method
- Clean the sprouts and blanch them.
- Cook until soft in salted water and leave to cool.
- Liquidise, heat in a suitable dish with the cream, finish with butter and season with salt and pepper.

Note A creamy purée can be obtained by using a whisk.

Purée d'haricots verts
Purée of French beans

Ingredients (for 4 people)
350g	(12oz)	haricots verts
		a little savory
5cl	(2fl oz)	double cream
20g	(¾oz)	butter
		salt, freshly ground white pepper

Method
- Clean the beans, cook in salted water with the savory until soft and allow to cool.
- Press through a very fine sieve, heat the purée with the cream and finish with butter.
- Season with salt and pepper.

Purée de marrons
Purée of chestnuts

Ingredients (for 4 people)

850g	(1¾lb)	chestnuts
50cl	(18fl oz)	milk
80g	(3¼oz)	butter
2cl	(¾fl oz)	Cognac
		sugar, salt

Method

- Split the chestnuts on the side with the tip of a knife, without piercing the inside.
- Lay on a baking tray and roast in a moderate oven for 5-7 minutes.
- Remove from the oven and discard the shells and the brown skin.
- Put the chestnuts into a saucepan and simmer for about 20 minutes with the milk.
- Press through a fine sieve.
- Put the purée into a suitable saucepan, reheat and mix in the butter with a wooden spoon.
- Season with salt, sugar and add Cognac to taste.

Note This purée goes very well with game. Cream may also be added at the end.

Subric d'épinards et de carottes
Carrot and spinach moulds

Ingredients (for 4 people)

200g	(7oz)	young carrots, peeled
5cl	(2fl oz)	double cream
20g	(¾oz)	butter
2cl	(¾fl oz)	white of 1½ eggs

▶

		salt, freshly ground white pepper
		a little sugar
350g	(12oz)	young spinach leaves, cleaned
10cl	(4fl oz)	double cream
2cl	(¾fl oz)	white of 1½ eggs

Method

- Cook the carrots until soft in a little salted water.
- Make into a purée, finish with cream and butter.
- Add the lightly beaten egg white.
- Season with salt, and a little sugar.
- Blanch the spinach leaves in salted water and dry well.
- Liquidise and mix in the cream.
- Add the lightly beaten egg white.
- Season with salt, white pepper and nutmeg.
- Pour equal quantities of the two mixtures into small buttered moulds and carefully poach in a bain-marie in the oven for 25-30 minutes.

Gratin de feuilles d'épinards
Gratin of leaf spinach

Ingredients (for 4 people)

600g	(1¼lb)	young fresh spinach leaves
10g	(½oz)	finely chopped shallot
30g	(1¼oz)	butter
100g	(4oz)	raw mushrooms, cut into slices
10cl	(4fl oz)	double cream
		salt, freshly ground white pepper
		a little nutmeg, freshly ground
40g	(1½oz)	freshly grated Emmental cheese

Method

- Blanch the washed spinach leaves (without their stems) in salt water, allow to cool and dry them. ▶

- Sweat the chopped shallot in butter and add the mushrooms.
- Add the spinach (without water) and mix in well.
- Add the cream and season with salt, pepper and nutmeg.
- Arrange in a greased gratin dish, add the cheese and top with butter.
- Place in the oven or under the grill until golden brown.

Note It is important that the spinach is lightly bound by the cream, i.e. without any liquid being left over.

Cooking and turning waste

In order to plan and cost the buying of vegetables, the wastage produced by cooking and turning must be included. $Cooking\ loss = C.L.\ Turning\ wastage = T.W.$

French	English	C.L.	T.W.
Pommes de terre	Potatoes	15%	20%
Carottes	Carrots	15%	15-20%
Chou-rave	Kohlrabi	15%	
Navets	Turnips	15%	15-20%
Petits oignons	Button onions	15%	
Betteraves	Beetroot	8%	
Échalotes	Shallots	12%	
Salsifis	Salsify	25-30%	
Céleri-rave	Celeriac	20-30%	15%
Oignons	Onions	10%	
Chou-fleur	Cauliflower	25-30%	
Chicorée belge	Endive	5%	
Fenouil	Fennel	15%	
Cardons	Cardoons	18%	
Laitue romaine	Cos lettuce	12%	
Poireaux	Leeks	12%	
Rhubarbe	Rhubarb	15%	
Choux de Bruxelles	Brussels sprouts	18-20%	
Chou-rouge, chou-blanc	Red cabbage, white cabbage	10%	
Céleri en branches	Celery	18%	
Asperges	Asparagus	40%	
Broccoli	Broccoli	50-70%	
Chou-vert	Green cabbage	15%	
Courgettes	Marrows	5%	
Tomates, epluchées, épépinées	Tomatoes, peeled, with pips removed	40%	

Chapter 12

Sweets

Sweets

Preserved fruit

Preserving fresh fruit is nothing new. Two years ago we re-introduced into the Dorchester Hotel the preserving of fruit in the old and trusted 'housewife's style' and a great many of our guests have taken a liking to it. We buy the fruit when it is in season, because then it is at its best, both in quality and flavour; it is also reasonable in price. For many months after we have a constant supply of a first class dessert which may be used in various ways.

The best way to serve the compôte is in the jar in which it has been sterilised, as a speciality of the house, so that the guest may make his own choice.

Fresh raspberry sauce or double cream makes a good accompaniment.

Here are a few simple rules:

- Only use first class, fresh, ripe fruit.
- Hygiene is the first responsibility so it is best to wear plastic gloves and the jars must be washed very thoroughly, then rinsed out in boiling water followed by cold water.
- The rubber ring around the top must be scalded too.
- Put the fruit carefully into the jars.
- Close the jars carefully.
- Sterilise in a steamer or in water.
- The sterilising time must be exactly adhered to.

Compôte de poires
Preserved pears

Ingredients

2kg	(4½lb)	pears, at their best (William or Comice)
1 litre	(1¾ pints)	water
500g	(18oz)	sugar
		lemon juice or pinch of vitamin C powder

Method (See Plate 17)

- Peel the pears carefully without removing the stalks.
- Remove the core with a Parisienne cutter.
- Lay the pears in water, flavoured with a little lemon juice, until needed.
- Blanch the pears in the lemon water and put them very carefully into the jars.
- Boil up the water and sugar, flavour with lemon juice or vitamin C powder and pour over the pears while still hot.
- Close the jars well and sterilise in a steamer for 8 to 10 minutes.

Note To give the pears more flavour, fresh mint leaves may be used.

Compôte de pêches
Preserved peaches

Ingredients

2.5kg	(5½lb)	medium sized peaches (with a good flavour)
1 litre	(1¾ pints)	water
500g	(18oz)	sugar
		lemon juice or pinch of vitamin C powder

Method (See Plate 17)

- Blanch the peaches in hot water, then plunge into cold water and finally peel them.
- Put the peaches carefully into the jars.
- Boil up the water and sugar, add lemon juice or vitamin C powder and pour over the fruit while still hot.
- Close the jars carefully and sterilise for 10-12 minutes in a steamer.

Compôte de cerises
Preserved cherries

Ingredients

3.5kg	(7¾lb)	white cherries
1 litre	(1¾ pints)	water
500g	(18oz)	sugar
		lemon juice or pinch of vitamin C powder

Method (See Plate 17)

- Remove the stalks from the cherries, wash them and then stone them.
- Boil up the water and sugar, flavour with lemon juice or vitamin C powder.

▶

- Put the cherries in the jars, add the hot syrup, close the jars carefully and sterilise for 5-6 minutes in a steamer.

Note The same method of preparation is also suitable for black cherries. To give the cherries more flavour a little cinnamon may be added.

Crêpes aux noisettes
Pancakes with chocolate and nut stuffing

Ingredients (for 4 people)

10cl	(4fl oz)	milk
60g	(2½oz)	flour
1		egg yolk
1		whole egg
15g	(¾oz)	sugar
10g	(½oz)	melted butter
10g	(½oz)	butter, for frying the pancakes

Method
- Put the milk and flour in a bowl and mix together well.
- Add the egg yolk, egg and sugar and mix in well.
- Add the melted butter and pass the mixture through a sieve.
- Fry very thin pancakes.

Filling

30g	(1¼oz)	macaroons, crushed
30g	(1¼oz)	hazelnuts } finely chopped
30g	(1¼oz)	walnuts
40cl	(¾ pint)	vanilla cream (see recipe 179)
20g	(¾oz)	sugar
50g	(2oz)	chocolate, melted

▶

1cl	(½fl oz)	Cognac
10cl	(4fl oz)	cream, whipped
2g		caster sugar

Method
- Mix the macaroons and nuts with the vanilla cream, sugar, chocolate and Cognac.
- Work in the whipped cream carefully.
- Fill the pancakes with this mixture, cover with butter paper and warm in the oven.
- Sprinkle with caster sugar just before serving.

Note It is a good idea to pour a little melted butter on to the pancakes before warming them in the oven.

Crème pâtissière
Vanilla cream

Ingredients (for 4 people)

25cl	(9fl oz)	milk
½		vanilla pod
3		egg yolks
80g	(3¼ oz)	sugar
40g	(1½oz)	flour

Method
- Bring the milk to the boil with the vanilla pod in a saucepan.
- Mix the egg yolks, sugar and flour together in a bowl.
- Add the boiling milk and mix in well.
- Return the mixture to the saucepan and bring to the boil slowly.
- Continue to boil for 2 to 3 minutes, stirring constantly.
- Strain through a fine sieve and keep warm until needed.

▶

Soufflé aux fruits de la passion
Passion fruit soufflé

Ingredients (for 4 people)

3		egg yolks
210g	(7½oz)	sugar
15cl	(¼ pint)	passion fruit juice
6		egg whites
5g	(¼oz)	butter

Method (See Plate 19)

- Beat together the egg yolks, half the sugar and two-thirds of the passion fruit juice.
- Whip together the egg whites and remaining sugar until creamy.
- Carefully add the egg whites to the egg yolks.
- Pour the mixture into a dish which has been buttered and dusted with sugar.
- Poach in a bain-marie for 7 or 8 minutes.
- Remove from the bain-marie and bake in an oven 170°-185° C (325°-350°F) for 25-30 minutes.
- For the sauce, boil up the remaining 5cl (2fl oz) passion fruit juice with 20g (¾oz) sugar and the juice of half a lemon and a little water, bind with a little Maizena, strain and serve lukewarm.

Note The rule here is that the guest must wait for the soufflé and not the soufflé for the guest. By pre-poaching in a bain-marie the cooking process can be somewhat drawn out. It is a good idea to serve half whipped cream alongside the sauce.

Ananas au poivre Jean et Pierre
Peppered pineapple with sauce of crème de Cacao

Jean and Pierre, the famous Troisgros brothers, are the namesake of this dish. I had the privilege to work with them for a few weeks, and experienced first hand the efficiency with which their hotel and restaurant kitchens run. *Les frères Troisgros* are amongst the most imaginative chefs in the world, which combined with their self-discipline and hospitality, makes them unforgettable and earns them a place in the evolution of French cooking.

Ingredients (for 4 people)

1		pineapple (about 320g (11oz))
		a little freshly ground black pepper
40g	(1½oz)	butter
3cl	(1fl oz)	crème de Cacao
4		portions of vanilla ice cream (see recipe 193)

Method (See Plate 20)
- Remove the skin of the pineapple.
- Cut into slices approximately 1cm (½in) thick and remove the middle core.
- Sprinkle the pineapple with the freshly ground pepper.
- Heat the butter in a pan, add the pineapple and flame with the crème de Cacao.
- Add the sauce (see below) and heat gently.
- Put the pineapple on to a plate and arrange the vanilla ice in the middle of each slice, then pour over the hot sauce.

▶

Sauce

100g	(4oz)	sugar
5cl	(2fl oz)	orange juice and zest
2cl	(¾fl oz)	lemon juice
5cl	(2fl oz)	crème de Cacao
25g	(1oz)	brown butter

Method

- Melt the sugar and let it become slightly brown (caramel).
- Add the orange and lemon juices.
- Add the crème de Cacao and reduce a little.
- Add the brown butter.
- Blanch the orange zest and add as garnish to the sauce.

Note This special dessert has a very pleasant aroma because of the combination of hot and cold. It is a good idea to prepare the dish in front of the guest.

Feuilleté aux framboises Eileen Atkins
Raspberries in puff pastry

This dish was created for Eileen Atkins, the famous actress, when she had dinner in one of the Dorchester's private dining rooms.

Ingredients (for 4 people)

200g	(7oz)	puff pastry (see recipe 19)
1		egg yolk, to glaze the pastry
		a little icing sugar
5cl	(2fl oz)	whipped cream
50g	(2oz)	vanilla cream (see recipe 179)
1cl	(½fl oz)	Himbeergeist (raspberry liqueur)
200g	(7oz)	raspberries, carefully selected and hulled
25cl	(9fl oz)	raspberry sauce (see recipe 183)
2cl	(¾fl oz)	half-whipped cream, for decoration

▶

Method (See Plate 18)
- Cut the puff pastry into 4 raspberry shapes. Mark a lid on each with a knife tip.
- Brush the shapes with egg yolk and bake them carefully in the oven at a fairly high temperature for 12-15 minutes.
- Remove the lids of the feuilletés, sprinkle with icing sugar and glaze in the oven.
- Mix the whipped cream with the warm vanilla cream and flavour with Himbeergeist.
- Fill the warm feuilletés with the crème, arrange the raspberries on top and put on the lid.
- Pour the raspberry sauce on to a plate and decorate the edge with the half-whipped cream (see picture).
- Place the feuilletés in the middle and serve immediately.

Note It is very important that these feuilletés are served warm.

Coulis de framboises
Raspberry sauce

Ingredients (for 25cl (9fl oz) sauce)
250g	(9 oz)	ripe raspberries
80g	(3¼ oz)	caster sugar
		juice of 1 lemon
		a little Himbeergeist (raspberry liqueur)

Method (See Plate 17)
- Purée the raspberries.
- Add the caster sugar.
- Flavour with the lemon juice and Himbeergeist.
- Strain the mixture through a fine sieve to remove the pips.

Note To ensure that this sauce has a fresh taste, it is very important to use only the freshest and ripest raspberries.

PLATE 18
Above: Assiette des sorbet Christine.
Plate of assorted sorbets (Recipe 200).

Right: Feuilleté aux framboises
Eileen Atkins. Raspberries in puff
pastry (Recipe 182).

PLATE 17 (Previous page)
Compôte de fruits et coulis de
framboises. Preserved fruits and
raspberry sauce (Recipes 175 to 177
and 183).

Gratin de pêches Marjorie
Gratinated peaches in pastry cream

Marjorie Lee has been in charge of public relations at the Dorchester for many, many years. Her knowledge is legendary — a walking "Who's Who"! She has done so much to make the Dorchester successful.

Ingredients (for 4 people)

4		white peaches (with a good flavour)
		a little Kirsch
		a little Curaçao
10g	(½oz)	Maizena or cornflour
30cl	(½ pint)	milk
60g	(2½oz)	sugar
2		egg yolks
15cl	(¼ pint)	whipped cream
60g	(2½oz)	brown sugar

Method

- Carefully peel the peaches and cut into thin slices.
- Arrange in a suitable round glass dish.
- Flavour with some of the Kirsch and Curaçao.
- Dissolve the Maizena in a little milk.
- Boil up the rest of the milk and bind with the Maizena.
- Mix together the egg yolks and sugar and stir in the boiling milk.
- Bring to the boil, strain and place in a bowl.
- Dust with sugar and allow to cool.
- When the mixture is cold, carefully work in the whipped cream and flavour with the remaining Kirsch and Curaçao.
- Cover the peaches with this crème, sprinkle with brown sugar and burn a glaze with a hot iron.

Note It is very important that the iron with which the sugar is burnt, is very hot so that a proper glaze of sugar forms. Yellow peaches, well ripened, may be used instead of the white ones.

Gratin au kiwi
Kiwi fruit au gratin

Ingredients (for 4 people)

6		kiwi fruit
5g	(¼oz)	butter
4		egg yolks
5cl	(2fl oz)	water
10g	(½oz)	vanilla sugar
40g	(1½oz)	sugar
20cl	(7fl oz)	double cream
2cl	(¾fl oz)	Kirsch

Method

- Carefully peel the kiwi fruit and cut attractively into slices.
- Arrange in a buttered gratin dish and stand this in a bain-marie.
- Beat the egg yolks, water, vanilla sugar and sugar well until a light airy mass is formed.
- Whip the cream until stiff and add to the mixture.
- Sprinkle the kiwi fruits with Kirsch and pour over the mixture.
- Poach in a bain-marie for about 25 minutes.
- Glaze in the oven or under the grill.
- Serve warm and offer a sorbet made from kiwi fruit as an accompaniment (see recipe 195).

Note The gratin should remain creamy inside and therefore should not be left too long under the grill. A kiwi fruit is also known as a Chinese gooseberry.

Strudel aux cerises
Homemade cherry strudel

Ingredients (for approx. 10 people)
For the dough

150g	(5 oz)	flour
2.5cl	(1 fl oz)	melted butter
6.5cl	(2½ fl oz)	lukewarm water
½		egg
		a pinch of salt

Method

- Make a well in the flour.
- Mix in the melted butter, water, egg and salt and knead into a firm dough.
- Allow to rest for an hour under a warm bowl.

Filling

30g	(1¼ oz)	melted butter, to brush on the dough
50g	(2 oz)	white breadcrumbs
20g	(¾ oz)	pine kernels
50g	(2 oz)	hazelnuts, finely ground
1kg	(2lb)	stoned cherries
150g	(5 oz)	cinnamon sugar
100g	(4 oz)	sultanas
30g	(1¼ oz)	butter for basting
		a little Kirsch

Method

- When the dough has rested, roll it into a rectangular shape, place on a cloth and stretch until quite thin.
- Brush the dough with melted butter and sprinkle with breadcrumbs, pine kernels, finely ground hazelnuts.
- Mix together the cherries, cinnamon sugar and sultanas and place on the dough. Add the Kirsch.
- Tuck in the ends of the dough and roll the whole mixture into a strudel. ▶

Recipe 186

- Place on a greased baking tray, brush with butter and bake at approx. 180°C (355°F) for 25-30 minutes, frequently basting with butter. It should be brown and crisp when done.

Note Only use fresh ripe cherries. Serve double cream separately.

Bread and butter pudding

Ingredients (for 4 people)

25cl	(9fl oz)	milk
25cl	(9fl oz)	double cream
		a little salt
1		vanilla pod
3		eggs
125g	(4½oz)	sugar
3		small bread rolls
30g	(1¼oz)	butter
10g	(½oz)	sultanas, soaked in water
20g	(¾oz)	apricot jam
		a little icing sugar

Method
- Bring the milk, cream, a little salt and the vanilla pod to the boil.
- Mix the eggs and sugar together.
- Add the simmering milk and cream.
- Pass the mixture through a sieve.
- Cut the rolls into thin slices and butter them. Arrange in a buttered ovenproof dish.
- Add the soaked raisins.
- Add the milk mixture, sprinkle the remaining butter on top and poach carefully for 35 to 40 minutes in a bain-marie.

▶

- Sprinkle with apricot jam and dust with icing sugar.

Note Bread and butter pudding may be served with double cream or bottled fruit.

Figues au coulis de framboises
Figs in raspberry sauce

Ingredients (for 4 people)

8		blue figs
400g	(14oz)	raspberries
150g	(5oz)	icing sugar
		juice of 1 lemon
		a little raspberry liqueur, preferably Himbeergeist
10cl	(4fl oz)	whipped cream
4		portions vanilla ice cream (see recipe 193)

Method
- Carefully peel the figs and cut into six pieces.
- Liquidise half of the raspberries and then pass through a fine sieve.
- Flavour with icing sugar, lemon juice and raspberry liqueur.
- Arrange this sauce on a flat plate and place the figs attractively on it.
- Garnish with whipped cream and raspberries.
- Serve the vanilla ice cream separately.

Note This dessert should be served as cold as possible.

Summer pudding

Ingredients (for 4 people)

8 to 10		slices of white bread with the crust removed
3g		gelatine leaves
10cl	(4fl oz)	water
150g	(5oz)	sugar
		juice of 1 lemon
100g	(4oz)	strawberries
100g	(4oz)	raspberries
100g	(4oz)	blackberries
10cl	(4fl oz)	raspberry sauce (see recipe 183)
20cl	(7fl oz)	double cream

} carefully selected and washed

Method

- Cut the slices of bread as shown (see opposite) and then place in a suitable pudding dish.
- Dissolve the gelatine leaves in water.
- Add the sugar and lemon juice and divide into three parts.
- Bring the strawberries, raspberries and blackberries quickly to the boil and simmer in the liquid in three separate pans.
- Allow to cool in the liquid.
- Arrange a layer of fruit alternately with a slice of bread in the pudding dish.
- Pour the rest of the liquid into the middle and cover with slices of bread.
- Press down with a weight and allow to rest for about 12 hours in the refrigerator.
- Turn out and coat with the raspberry sauce.
- Serve the double cream separately.

Note The fruits may be varied according to availability.

Stages in making
Summer Pudding, as
described in Recipe
189.

Recipe 189

Crêpe sans rival
Pancake with a cream and fruit filling

Pancake recipe as for recipe 178.

Filling

20cl	(7fl oz)	vanilla cream (see recipe 179)
30g	(1¼oz)	hazelnuts, finely ground
40g	(1½oz)	marzipan
1cl	(½fl oz)	Pernod
4		kiwi fruits, peeled and thinly cut

Garnish

15cl	(¼ pint)	meringage à l'italienne (see recipe 191)
20g	(¾oz)	hazelnuts, finely ground
20cl	(7fl oz)	raspberry sauce (see recipe 183)
		kiwi fruits thinly sliced

Method (See Plate 20)

- Mix the vanilla cream with the finely ground hazelnuts and the marzipan.
- Finish with the Pernod.
- Spread this mixture thinly on the pancakes.
- Lay some of the finely cut kiwi fruits in the middle.
- Fold the pancakes over from both sides.
- Garnish with the meringage à l'italienne, to which 20g (¾oz) of the ground hazelnuts has been added.
- Bake the pancakes in a warm oven for 4-5 minutes.
- Pour some raspberry sauce on to a plate and place the pancakes on it.
- Garnish with finely sliced kiwi fruits.
- Serve immediately.

Note The special point about this sweet is that the pancakes must be served hot and the filling cold. The fruit may be varied according to season, for instance white or yellow peaches may be used.

Meringage à l'italienne
Italian meringue mixture

Ingredients

100g	(4oz)	sugar
5cl	(2 fl oz)	water
2		egg whites
20g	(¾ oz)	icing sugar

Method

- Place and heat the sugar and water in a heavy pan and stir until the sugar is dissolved.
- Cook until the syrup reaches 100-115°C (210-240°F).
- Meanwhile, beat the egg whites until stiff and fold in the icing sugar.
- Add the cooked syrup slowly (in threads) to the beaten egg whites.
- Continue beating until the mixture is cool.

Pêches à la glace de pistache
Peach with pistachio ice cream

Ingredients (for 4 people)

4		medium sized ripe peaches
10cl	(4 fl oz)	Sherry
150g	(5 oz)	sugar
½		vanilla pod
		water

Method

- Blanch and peel the peaches.　　　►

- Make a syrup out of the Sherry, sugar, vanilla and a little water.
- Poach the peaches in the liquid and allow to cool.

Ice cream

15cl	(¼ pint)	milk
15cl	(¼ pint)	double cream
50g	(2 oz)	sugar
50g	(2 oz)	pistachio nuts, finely chopped
3		egg yolks

Method

- Bring half the milk, cream, sugar and pistachio nuts to the boil.
- Mix the egg yolks with the other half of the milk and add to the boiling mixture.
- Pass the mixture through a sieve, put into moulds and freeze.

Sauce

150g	(5 oz)	whole rose hips
20g	(¾ oz)	redcurrant jelly
20g	(¾ oz)	sugar
5cl	(2fl oz)	red wine

Method

- Remove the pips from the rose hips and wash well.
- Boil the rose hips with the redcurrent jelly, sugar and red wine for 20 minutes.
- Arrange the peaches on top of the ice cream and cover with sauce.
- Serve with freshly baked petits fours (see recipes 201 and 202).

Glace à la vanille
Vanilla ice cream

Ingredients (for 4 people)

4		egg yolks
150g	(5 oz)	sugar
25cl	(9fl oz)	milk
25cl	(9fl oz)	double cream
½		vanilla pod, cut lengthwise

Method
- Mix the egg yolks well with the sugar.
- Gradually add the hot milk and cream.
- Put the mixture into a saucepan. Add the vanilla pod.
- Bring the mixture to just before boiling point, stirring constantly (this point is reached when, after removing the spatula from the mixture and running one's finger along it, the mixture remains separated).
- Immediately remove from the heat and allow to cool in a cold bain-marie, stirring occasionally.
- Strain through a fine sieve and freeze.

Sorbets

Sorbets made from fresh fruit at its best are amongst the most popular sweets. They taste best without anything added (alcohol or egg white). Sorbets must be fresh and should not be made in advance, otherwise the fruit aroma is lost. To make them richer, sorbets may be served with fresh fruit of the season.

Note The sugar content of fruit varies according to the season, so it is important that the fruit and sugar are checked and brought up to 17° Baumé by means of a saccharometer. The Baumé scale measures the degree of sweetness of a product — the highest being 28° Baumé the lowest being 1°.

700g of sugar in 1 litre of boiling water gives about 17° Baumé.

Sorbet au melon
Melon sorbet

Ingredients (for approx. 4 people)

400g	(14 oz)	melon (Ogen), with a good flavour
100g	(4oz)	sugar
		juice of 1 lemon

Method
- Cut the melon in half and remove the seed with a spoon.
- Carefully peel the melon and cut into pieces.
- Liquidise the pieces of melon.
- Add the sugar and lemon juice, stir in well, freeze and store in a sorbetière.

Note Other types of melon may be used, depending on the season.

Sorbet au kiwi
Kiwi sorbet with Champagne

Ingredients (for 4 people)

800g	(1¾lb)	kiwi fruit
10cl	(4 fl oz)	water
20cl	(7fl oz)	Champagne
150g	(5 oz)	sugar
5g	(¼ oz)	vanilla sugar
		juice of ½ lemon
		a little Pernod

Method
- Peel the well ripened kiwis and liquidise them. ▶

- Boil up the water, Champagne, sugar and vanilla sugar and add to the purée of kiwi fruit
- Cover and allow to cool, finish with lemon juice and Pernod.
- Pass the mixture through a fine sieve.
- Freeze and store in a sorbetière.

Note A kiwi fruit is also known as a Chinese gooseberry.

Sorbet à l'orange sanguine
Blood orange sorbet

Ingredients (for 4 people)

500g	(18 oz)	juicy, blood oranges
10		cubes of sugar
1 cl	(½ fl oz)	lemon juice
150g	(5 oz)	sugar

Method
- Wash the oranges well.
- Rub off the orange peel with the lumps of sugar.
- Boil up the lemon juice with the lumps of sugar.
- Cut the oranges in half and squeeze out the juice.
- Mix the orange and lemon juice and the sugar together and pass through a fine sieve.
- Freeze and store in a sorbetière.

Note By rubbing the orange peel with the cubes of sugar, a stronger orange taste is obtained.

Sorbet à l'ananas
Pineapple sorbet

Ingredients (for 4 people)

1		ripe pineapple (about 500g (18oz))
		juice of 1 lemon
120g	(4½ oz)	sugar

Method
- Peel the pineapple.
- Cut the pineapple flesh (without the centre) into small pieces.
- Liquidise and then pass through a fine sieve.
- Add the lemon juice and sugar and stir well.
- Freeze and store in a sorbetière.

Note Depending on the origin and quality of the pineapple, the sugar content must be checked (see page 288).

Sorbet à la framboise
Raspberry sorbet

Ingredients (for 4 people)

250g	(9 oz)	raspberries
100g	(4 oz)	sugar
		juice of ½ lemon

Method
- Select the raspberries carefully.
- Liquidise and pass through a fine sieve.
- Add the sugar and lemon juice and stir in well.
- Freeze and store in a sorbetière.

Note The addition of sugar varies according to season.

Sorbet à la mangue
Mango sorbet

Ingredients (for 4 people)

25cl	(9fl oz)	mango purée
5cl	(2 fl oz)	water
100g	(4 oz)	sugar
2g		fresh ginger, finely grated
		juice of 1 lemon

Method
- Prepare the mango purée, as for the other sorbets and boil up with water, sugar and fresh ginger.
- Strain, finish with the lemon juice and leave to cool.
- Freeze and store in a sorbetière.

Note It is advisable to use only completely ripe mangoes.

Assiette des sorbets Christine

This dish is named after Christine Guérard, the lovely wife of one of the most famous chefs in the world, and certainly one of the most creative being the founder of *Cuisine Minceur*. I was fortunate enough to have an opportunity to work with Michel Guérard for a couple of months, during which time I picked up many hints from this master of creativity.

A selection of five different sorbets according to the fruit in season, garnished with appropriate fresh fruit. (See Plate 18).

Petits fours aux noix
Walnut petits fours

Ingredients (for 50 biscuits)

125g	(4½ oz)	butter
75g	(3 oz)	icing sugar
		zest of 1 lemon
1		egg
1		egg yolk
90g	(3½ oz)	ground hazelnuts
125g	(4½ oz)	flour
		a pinch of cinnamon
50		halved walnuts to top biscuits

Method

- Cream the butter and icing sugar with the lemon zest.
- Mix in the egg and the yolk.
- Fold in the hazelnuts, flour and cinnamon.
- Pipe out with a No. 11 star tube on to a lightly greased oven tray into rosettes and place half a walnut on each.
- Bake at about 190°C (375°F), then allow to cool.
- When cool, half dip in chocolate couverture.

'A wife who is a good cook can be her husband's first Minister of State. A wife who can cook need never fear the "other woman" — unless, of course, the other woman is a better cook!'

PLATE 20
Above: Crêpe sans rival. Pancake with a cream and fruit filling *(Recipe 190).*

Left: Ananas au poivre Jean et Paul. Peppered pineapple with sauce of crème de Cacao *(Recipe181).*

PLATE 19 (Previous page)
Above: Soufflé aux fruits de la passion. Passion fruit soufflé *(Recipe 180).*

Petits fours Florentine

Ingredients (for 50 pieces)

200g	(7 oz)	sugar paste (see recipe 20)
5cl	(2 fl oz)	double cream
40g	(1½ oz)	butter
40g	(1½ oz)	honey
110g	(4¼ oz)	sugar
20g	(¾ oz)	glucose
100g	(4 oz)	mixed fruit peel
60g	(2½ oz)	nibbed almonds
60g	(2½ oz)	flaked almonds

Method

- Roll out the sugar paste to a 15cm (6 inch) ring, prick the paste with a fork, and part bake it.
- Boil in a copper bowl the cream, butter, honey, sugar and glucose to 110°C (230°F).
- Stir in the peel and almonds.
- Spread this on the sugar paste and bake at 180°C (350°F) until golden brown.

Glossary of Terms

Al dente   Usually applied to vegetables and pasta dishes which are slightly undercooked so that they are just biteable or crunchy. The French term *croquant* is perhaps more descriptive.

A la minute   Making something to order.

Barder   Barding — to cover poultry or game with slice of bacon before roasting so that the breast meat does not dry out too much during roasting.

Bouquet garni   A mixture of parsley stalks, bay leaf, peppercorns and thyme wrapped with celeriac and carrots tied together.

    A white bouquet garni consists only of onion, white of leek and celeriac plus herbs. It is used for white stocks.

Brunoise   Small dice of vegetables.

Clarifier   To clarify a liquid; the term is usually applied to clear soup such as bouillon which is clarified with white of egg to remove the last vestiges of meat. The result is a brilliantly clear consommé. The term is also used with butter: clarified butter is melted so that the solids and the liquid are separated out. Clarified butter has a higher burning point and will not caramelize or burn so easily as unclarified butter.

Coulis   A liquid purée of fruit or vegetables, made without flour, but a coulis of meat or fish is possible.

Court-bouillon	Stock for poaching fish or other seafoods (see recipe 7).
Crèpine	The caul or lining of a pig's stomach (see recipes 116 & 153).
Emincer	Cut into small slices.
Farce	A mixture of meat, poultry, fish or vegetables used for stuffing (*farcir* is the French verb to stuff).
Feuilletés	Puff pastry cases cut into different shapes.
Fleurons	Small cuts of puff pastry, usually half-moon shape.
Fond	A basic stock used for soups and sauces (see recipes 1-6).
Fritreuse	Deep fat fryer.
Fruits-de-mer	All kinds of seafood, crustaceans and molluscs.
Fumet	A rich liquid prepared by cooking foods (usually fish) in stock and/or wine. The liquid is reduced (boiled off so that much of it evaporates) to make it stronger.
Glace de viande	A meat glaze, prepared by reducing a good basic veal or beef stock (see recipe 9).
Julienne	Meat or vegetables cut into fine strips not longer than the width of a soupspoon.
Marmite	A double size stock pot. A marmite is also a strong, clear broth with vegetables, meat or chicken.
Mariner	To marinate or to place in a marinade which can consist of wine (or vinegar), vegetables and herbs as appropriate.
Monter au beurre	To mix carefully hard butter cut in pieces into a sauce to thicken the liquid.

Mirepoix	Dice of vegetables (size according to the need; consisting usually of carrots, onions, turnips and herbs — but other vegetables may be used.
Napper	To coat foods evenly with a sauce or aspic jelly, or to cover the surface of a serving dish.
Papillote	Literally, an envelope. Used in cookery to describe the wrapping of meat or fish in tin foil or greaseproof paper, in which the meat or fish is baked (see recipe 77).
Paupiettes	Stuffed and rolled slices of meat or fillets of fish.
Quenelles	Dumplings of meat, fish, poultry or game made by finely mincing the meat, adding seasoning and mixing with cream and maybe egg white. The quenelles are poached in salt water or in a strong stock as appropriate.
Salamander	A grill with heat from above.
Sorbetière	Container for ice cream, sorbets and other ices.
Sauteuse	Small sauté pan.
Sautoir	Large sauté pan.
Tronçon	A thick slice of a small fish, but it can refer to a piece of the tail of a large fish.
Zest	The grated peel of citrus fruits.

Index

Aiguillettes de canard sauvage Albert Schnell, 162
Almonds, with breast of pheasant, 157
Ananas au poivre Jean et Pierre, 181
Anguilles vertes, 103
Artichoke:
    purée, 168
    salad with quails, 38
Asparagus:
    green, with haddock fillets, 93
    with lobster salad, 37
Assiette des sorbets Christine, 200
Aubergines in *Trianon de légumes*, 166
Avocado salad, with mushrooms, 41

Bananas, with breast of chicken, 148
Basil:
    butter, 33
    sauce, with seafood, 104
Beans, French, purée of, 171
Beef:
    fillet, with chicken mousseline and Madeira sauce, 116
    fillet, with meat marrow and red wine sauce, 118
    grilled rib, with herbs and butter sauce, 121
    liver quenelles, with double consommé, 62
    mignons, with red wine sauce and chopped shallots, 120
    sirloin steak in cream sauce with four different peppers, 115
    strips, in cream sauce with green peppercorns, 117
Beetroot mousseline, 169
Beurre:
    de basilic, 33
    d'écrevisses, 35
    de pistache, 34
Billy Bye soup, 68
Biscuit de barbue à la crème d'oursins, 98
Blanc de turbot parfumé à la moutarde, 88
Blanc de volaille sous cloche, 144
Blanquette d'agneau au safron, 127
Bouillon de viande, 11

Bread and butter pudding, 187
Bread sauce, 159
Brill mousse, with sea-urchin sauce, 98
Brioche navigateur, 114
Brioche:
    paste, 17
    with seafood and mushrooms, 114
Broth:
    meat, 11
    Scotch, 63
    (*see also* Consommé; Soup)
Brussels sprouts, mousseline of, 170
Butter:
    basil, 33
    crayfish, 35
    pistachio, 34
Butter sauce:
    with grilled rib of beef and herbs, 121
    scallops in, 106

Calves' liver with onions and Madeira sauce, 139
Calves' sweetbreads:
    with spinach, 135
    steamed, with truffles, vegetables and cream sauce, 136
Carrot and spinach moulds, 173
Carrot leaf sauce, with steamed baby chicken, 148
Cassolette de moules au fenouil, 113
Caviar:
    with eggs in cocotte, 75
    with oysters and Champagne sauce, 59
Célestine de boeuf au poivre vert, 117
Champagne:
    and kiwi sorbet, 195
    sauce, with oysters and caviar, 59
Chanterelle soup, 64
Cherries, preserved, 177
Cherry strudel, homemade, 186
Chestnuts, purée of, 172
Chicken:
    baby, grilled with vegetables, 149
    baby, steamed with carrot leaf sauce, 148

breast, stuffed with mango, 143
breast, with banana, 147
breast, in puff pastry, 145
breast, with mushroom sauce, 144
forcemeat, with Terrine Covent Garden, 45
fricassée with vinegar sauce, 152
liver parfait with truffles, 51
with mixed peppers, 150
mousseline, 15
mousseline, with fillet of beef and Madeira
    sauce, 116
sautéd, with crayfish, 150
with terrine and sweetbreads, 48
Chives:
    with fillets of perch and vegetables, 100
    with fresh river trout, 81
    sauce, scallops in, 107
Chocolate and nut filling, with pancakes, 178
Coeur de filet de boeuf soufflé, 116
Compôte de cerises, 177
Compôte de pêches, 176
Compôte de poires, 175
Consommé, double, with liver quenelles, 62
    (*see also* Broth; Soup; Stock)
Coquelet à la vapeur, 148
Coquilles St. Jacques:
    à la crème de ciboulette, 107
    au beurre blanc, 106
    au safran, 108
    galloises, 56
    mousseline de, 57
    soupe de, Maître Camille, 70
Côte de boeuf marinée aux herbes du jardin,
    121
Côte de veau sauté aux morilles farcies, 131
Coulis de framboises, 183
Courgettes in Trianon de légumes, 166
Court-bouillon, 7
Crabmeat, terrine, with sorrel sauce, 111
Crayfish:
    butter, 35
    with sautéd chicken, 151
    sauce, 24
    tails gratinated with hollandaise sauce, 112
    tart, 53
    with turbot soufflé, 87
Cream and fruit filling, with pancakes, 190
Cream sauce:
    sirloin steak in, with four different peppers,
        115
    mignons of veal in, with sorrel, 129
    strips of beef in, with green peppercorns,
        117
    strips of veal with mixed mushrooms, 133
Crème de Cacao sauce, 181
Crème pâtissière, 179
Crêpes:
    aux noisettes, 178

de maïs, 167
sans rival, 190
Curry sauce, 32

Délice de volaille farci à la banane, 147
Dublin Bay prawns Maître Gilgen, 58
Duck:
    breast, grilled with green peppercorns, 153
    fillets of wild, with juniper berry sauce, 162
    liver terrine, 49
    wild duck stock, 12
Duo de cailles farcies au riz sauvage, 160

Écrevisses au gratin, 112
Eels in herb sauce, 103
Eggs:
    in cocotte, with caviar, 75
    lobster, with raw sea bass, 43
    poached, with marinated Scottish salmon,
        71
    quails', with clear quail soup, 60
    quails', with creamed leek, 73
    scrambled, with frogs' legs, 76
    soft boiled, with sweetbreads and mush-
        rooms, 74
Elixir de cailles aux oeufs, 61
Emincé de veau belle forestière, 133
Entrecôte sautée Dorchester, 115
Epigramme de flétan 'Maître Jules', 91
Epinards en feuilles, 125
Escalope de truite saumonée aux poireaux
    (2 versions), 78, 79

Farce au gratin, 16
Farce de volaille, 45
Fennel sauce, mussels in, 113
Feuilleté aux framboises Eileen Atkins, 182
Figs in raspberry sauce, 188
Figues au coulis de framboises, 188
Filet de flétan en laitue, 92
Filet de rouget à la vapeur sous cloche, 99
Filet de turbot aux huîtres, 90
Filet de veau poêlé au foie gras, 134
Filets de St Pierre sans nom, 97
Filets des danseuses de rivière à la ciboulette,
    81
Filets des percheaux aux petites légumes, 100
Fish:
    court-bouillon for, 7

soup with chervil, 69
stock, 6
Florentines, 202
Foie gras: see Goose liver
Foie de veau vénitienne, 139
Fond(s):
blanc de veau, 2
blanc de volaille, 1
brun de veau, 4
brun de volaille, 3
d'agneau, 5
de gibier, 10
de légumes, 13
de moules, 8
de poisson, 6
Forcemeat, for game, 16
chicken, 45
Foyot sauce, 31
Fricassée de volaille au vinaigre, 152
Frogs' legs:
in puff pastry, 52
with scrambled eggs, 76

Game:
forcemeat for, 16
sauce, 29
with medallions of venison, 155
with roast saddle of hare, 156
stock, 10
Gigot d'agneau farci en croûte, 122
Glace(s):
de pistache, 192
de vanille, 193
Glace de viande, 9
Goose liver:
with fillet of veal, 134
fresh, with red wine and shallots, 54
salad, French, 39
terrine, mixed spices for, 50
Goujons de sole aux oranges et poivres verts,
85
Goujons de turbot au safran, 89
Grapes:
with fillet of halibut, 91
with partridge in pastry, 161
Gratin au kiwi, 185
Gratin de feuilles d'épinards, 174
Gratin de pêches Marjorie, 184
Green sauce, with monkfish, 94
Grenadins de baudroie à la sauce verte, 94
Grouse rôti à l'écossaise, 158
Grouse, roast Scottish, 158
Guinea fowl:
breast, with black and green olives, 146
sauce, 146

Haddock fillets with green asparagus, 93
Halibut fillet:
in lettuce leaves, 92
with seafood and grapes, 91
Hare, roast saddle, with game sauce, 156
Herb(s):
fresh, with grilled monkfish tail, 95
with grilled beef cutlet and butter sauce, 121
mixture, 123
sauce, with eels, 103
Herring terrine with dill, 47
Huîtres moscovite au Champagne, 59

Ice cream:
pistachio, 192
vanilla, 193
(see also Sorbet*)*
Italian meringue mixture, 191

John Dory, fillets, in white wine sauce with
tomatoes, 97
Juniper berry sauce, with wild duck fillets,
162

Kidneys:
veal, in mustard sauce, 138
veal, in red wine vinegar sauce, 137
Kiwi fruit au gratin, 185
Kiwi sorbet with Champagne, 195

Lamb:
blanquette, with saffron sauce, 127
mignons, with Port wine sauce, 124
poached saddle, with vegetables, 126
stock, 5
stuffed leg, in pastry, 122
Leek(s):
creamed, with quails' eggs, 73
sauce, with salmon trout (2 versions), 78, 79
with scallops fried in butter, 56
soup with white wine, 65
Lentilles braisées (Lentils, braised), 165
Liver: *(see also* Goose liver*)*
calves', with onions and Madeira sauce, 139
chicken liver parfait with truffles, 51

duck, terrine, 49
quenelles, with double consommé, 62
Lobster:
   eggs, with raw sea bass, 43
   salad with asparagus, 37
   sauce, 23
      with green noodles and seafood, 105
   sole and, timbale Eugène Käufeler, 83
   with timbale of pike and spinach, 102
Loup de mer cru aux oeufs de homard, 43

Madeira sauce, 30
   with calves' liver and onions, 139
   with fillet of beef and chicken mousseline,
     116
Màgret de canard grillé — Nossi-Bé, 153
Mango:
   chicken breast stuffed with, 143
   sorbet, 199
Marrow, with turbot fillets, 86
Meat:
   broth, 11
   glaze, 9
Meat marrow, with fillet of beef, 118
Médaillons de chevreuil belle forestière, 155
Médaillons de filet de porc au Roquefort, 141
Médaillons de filet de porc sauce Western,
   140
Médaillons de foie gras au vin rouge, 54
Médaillons de porc aux pruneaux, 142
Médaillons de veau à l'orange et citron, 130
Mélange d'épices pour foie gras, 50
Méli-mélo de homard aux pointes d'asperges,
   37
Melon sorbet, 194
Meringage à l'italienne, 191
Mignons d'agneau au Porto, 124
Mignons de boeuf aux échalotes, 120
Mignons de chevreuil à la purée de persil, 154
Mignons de veau à l'oseille, 129
Monkfish:
   with green sauce, 94
   tail, with black peppercorns, 96
   tail, grilled, with fresh herbs, 95
Morels, stuffed, with veal cutlets, 131
Morilles farcies, 132
Mousseline de betterave, 169
Mousseline de brochet, 14
Mousseline de choux de Bruxelles, 170
Mousseline de coquilles St. Jacques, 57
Mousseline de volaille, 15
Mullet: *see* Red mullet
Mushroom(s):
   with avocado salad, 41
   with brioche and seafood, 114

with homemade ravioli and tomatoes, 55
sauce, with breast of chicken, 144
with sautéd medallions of venison, 155
with soft boiled eggs and sweetbreads, 74
with veal in cream sauce, 133
Mussel(s):
   Billy Bye soup, 68
   in fennel sauce, 113
   stock, 8
Mustard sauce:
   with turbot fillets, 88
   veal kidneys in, 137

Nouilles aux épinards, 22
Nouilles vertes aux fruits-de-mer, 105
Noodles:
   green, with fillet of veal and cheese, 128
   green, with seafood in lobster sauce, 105
   homemade egg, with spinach, 22

Oeufs brouillés aux cuisses de grenouilles, 76
Oeufs de cailles aux poireaux, 73
Oeufs en cocotte au caviar, 75
Oeufs mollets au ragoût fin, 74
Oeufs pochés aux délice de saumon mariné,
   71
Olives with breast of guinea fowl, 160
Orange(s):
   and lemons, with veal medallions, 130
   blood orange sorbet, 196
   with goujons of sole, 85
Oyster(s):
   with caviar and Champagne sauce, 59
   with fillet of turbot and julienne of
     vegetables, 90
   salad with spinach, 40

Pancakes:
   with a cream and fruit filling, 190
   with chocolate and nut stuffing, 178
   with creamed sweetcorn, 167
Parfait de foies de volaille aux truffes, 51
Parsley purée, with mignons of venison, 154
Partridge with grapes in pastry, 161
Passion fruit soufflé, 180
Paste (pastry):
   brioche, 17
   puff, 19
   ravioli, 21, 55

shortcrust, 18
sugar, 20
(*see also* Puff pastry)
Pastry cream, gratinated peaches in, 184
Pâte:
  à ravioli, 21
  sucrée, 20
  brisée, 18
  de brioche, 17
  feuilletée, 19
Paupiettes de sole Montrose, 84
Peach(es):
  gratinated, in pastry cream, 184
  with pistachio ice cream, 192
  preserved, 176
Pears, preserved, 175
Pêches à la glace de pistache, 192
Peppercorns:
  black, with monkfish tail, 96
  green, with goujons of sole and oranges, 85
  green, with grilled duck's breast, 153
Perch fillets, with vegetables and chives, 100
Perdreau rôti aux raisins de muscat, 161
Pernod sauce, with scampi, 105
Petits fours aux noix, 201
Petits fours Florentine, 202
Pheasant:
  breast, with almonds, 157
  sauce, 157
Piccata de veau Cavalieri, 128
Pike:
  mousseline, 14, 87
  poached quenelles 'Mère Olga', 101
  timbale, with spinach and lobster, 102
Pineapple:
  peppered, with sauce of crème de Cacao, 181
  sorbet, 197
Pistachio:
  butter, 34
  ice cream, with peach, 192
Pollo alla Romana, 150
Poésie de cuisses de grenouilles au Riesling, 52
Pommes à l'ail gratinées, 164
Pommes Maison, 163
Pork:
  fillets in Roquefort sauce, 141
  fillet of, medallions with prunes, 142
  fillet of, medallions with Western sauce, 140
Port wine sauce, with lamb mignons, 124
Potage:
  aux chanterelles, 64
  aux escargots, 66
  aux quenelles de foie, 62
  de légumes froid, 61
  Pigalle, 65
Potatoes home-style, 163

Potato, gratin of, with cream and garlic, 164
Poulet sautée aux écrevisses, 151
Poultry:
  brown stock, 3
  white stock, 1
  (*see also* Chicken)
Poussin aux légumes grillés, 149
Prawns:
  Dublin Bay, 58
  with fillets of sole and white wine sauce, 82
Prunes, with pork medallions, 142
Puff pastry, 19
  breast of chicken in, 152
  frogs' legs in, 52
  lightning, 19
  partridge with grapes in, 161
  raspberries in, 182
  stuffed leg of lamb in, 122
Purée d'artichauts, 168
Purée d'haricots verts, 171
Purée de marrons, 172

Quail(s):
  with artichoke salad, 38
  clear soup, with soft egg, 60
  stuffed, with wild rice, 160
Quails' eggs:
  with clear quail soup, 60
  with creamed leeks, 73
Quenelles de brochet 'Mère Olga', 101
Quenelles:
  liver, with double consommé, 62
  poached pike 'Mere Olga', 101
Queue de lotte au poivre noir, 96
Queue de lotte grillée aux herbes, 95

Râble de lièvre rôti au sang, 156
Raspberries in puff pastry, 182
Raspberry sauce, 183
Raspberry sorbet, 198
Ravioli alla Casalinga, 55
Ravioli:
  homemade with mushrooms and tomatoes, 55
  paste, 21
Red mullet fillets with vinaigrette sauce, 99
Red wine sauce, 119
  with fillet of beef and meat marrow, 118
  with mignons of beef and chopped shallots, 120
  with shallots, 28
Red wine vinegar sauce, veal kidneys in, 137
Rendez-vous de fruits-de-mer à la crème de basilic, 104

Rice (wild) stuffing, 160
Ris de veau aux feuilles d'épinards, 135
Ris de veau piqués à la vapeur, 136
Rognons de veau à la moutarde, 138
Rognons de veau au vinaigre de vin, 137
Roquefort sauce, with pork fillets, 141
Rose hips sauce, with peach, 192
Rosette de boeuf Grand Hôtel, 118
Rosette de saumon fumé au mousse de truite
    Dorchester, 42

Saffron:
    with goujons of turbot, 89
    sauce, with blanquette of lamb, 127
    sauce, with scallops, 108
Salad(s):
    artichoke, with quails, 38
    avocado, with mushrooms, 41
    French goose liver, 39
    lobster, with asparagus, 37
    oyster, with spinach, 40
Salade d'avocats, 41
Salade aux huîtres Catherine, 40
Salade de foie gras moderne, 39
Salmon:
    marinated Scottish, 72
    marinated Scottish, with poached eggs, 71
    soufflé with pike mousseline, 80
    steak papillote-style, 77
    (see also Smoked salmon)
Salmon trout with leek (2 versions), 78, 79
Sauce(s):
    au curry, 32
    aux écrevisses, 24
    aux truffles, 27
    Foyot, 31
    homard, 23
    hollandaise, 26
    madère, 30
    marchand de vin, 28
    'Mère Olga', 101
    verte, 94
    vin rouge, 119
    vinaigrette, 37, 39, 40, 99
    Western, 25, 140
Sauce(s):
    basil, 104
    bread, 159
    butter, 106, 121
    carrot leaf, 148
    Champagne, 59
    chive, 107
    crayfish, 24
    cream, 115, 117, 129, 133, 136
    crème de Cacao, 181
    curry, 32
    fennel, 113

for fillets of John Dory, 97
Foyot, 31
game, 29, 155, 156
green, 94
guinea fowl, 146
herb, 103
hollandaise, 26, 112
juniper berry, 162
leek, 78
lobster, 23
'Mere Olga', 101
for mousseline scallops, 57
mushroom, 144
mustard, 88, 138
Pernod, 110
pheasant, 157
Port wine, 124
raspberry, 183
ravioli, 55
red wine, 28, 119, 120
red wine vinegar, 137
Roquefort, 141
rose hips, 192
saffron, 108, 127
sea-urchin, 98
sorrel, 111
sour cream and mustard, 71
for timbale of pike, 102
truffle, 27
vinaigrette, 37, 39, 40, 99
Western, 25, 140
white wine, 82
white wine vinegar, 152
Saumon d'Écosse Maître Schlegel, 80
Saumon d'Écosse mariné, 72
Scallop(s):
    in butter sauce, 106
    in chives sauce, 107
    fried in butter with leeks, 56
    mousseline, with fresh tomato purée, 57
    with saffron sauce, 108
    soup with julienne of vegetables, 70
Scampi amoureuse, 110
Scampie sautés Maître Cola, 109
Scampi:
    sautéd with artichokes, 109
    with Pernod sauce, 110
Scotch broth, 63
Scottish salmon: see Salmon
Sea bass, raw, with lobster eggs, 43
Seafood:
    in basil sauce, 104
    with brioche and mushrooms, 114
    with fillet of halibut, 91
    in lobster sauce, with green noodles, 105
Sea-urchin sauce, 98
Selle d'agneau pochée aux légumes, 126
Sirloin steak in cream sauce with 4 different
    peppers, 115

Smoked salmon:
   with paupiettes of sole, 84
   with trout mousse Dorchester-style, 42
Snail(s):
   preparation of, 67
   soup with vermouth, 66
Sole:
   fillets, with white wine sauce and prawns, 82
   goujons of, with oranges and green peppercorns, 85
   and lobster timbale Eugène Käufeler, 83
   paupiettes of, with smoked salmon, 84
Sorbet:
   à l'ananas (pineapple), 197
   à l'orange de sanguine (blood orange), 196
   à la framboise (raspberry), 198
   au kiwi, 195
   à la mangue (mango), 199
   au melon, 194
Sorrel:
   sauce, with terrine of crabmeat, 111
   with veal steaks in cream sauce, 129
Soufflé aux fruits de la passion, 180
Soufflé:
   passion fruit, 180
   salmon, 80
   turbot, with crayfish, 87
Soup:
   Billy Bye, 68
   chanterelle, 64
   clear quail, with soft egg, 60
   cold vegetable, with basil, 61
   fish, with chervil, 69
   leek, with white wine, 65
   scallop, with julienne of vegetables, 70
   snail, with vermouth, 66
   (see also Broth; Consommé; Stock)
Soupe de coquilles St. Jacques Maître Camille, 70
Soupe de poisson de mer, 69
Spices, mixed, for goose or duck, 50
Spinach:
   with calves' sweetbreads, 135
   and carrot moulds, 173
   with homemade egg noodles, 22
   leaf, 125
   leaf, gratin of, 174
   with oyster salad, 40
   with timbale of pike, 102
Steak de saumon en papillotes, 77
Stock:
   brown poultry, 3
   brown veal, 4
   court-bouillon, 7
   fish, 6
   game, 10
   guinea fowl, 146
   lamb, 5

   lobster, 37
   mussel, 8
   oyster, 40
   vegetable, 13
   white poultry, 1
   white veal, 2
   wild duck, 12
   (see also Broth; Soup)
Strudel aux cerises, 186
Stuffing:
   chicken forcemeat, for Terrine Covent Garden, 45
   game forcemeat, 16
   wild rice, with quails, 160
Subrics d'épinards et de carottes, 173
Sugar paste, 20
Summer pudding, 189
Suprême d'aiglefin Elysée, 93
Suprême de faisan aux amandes, 157
Suprême de pintadeaux aux olives noirs et vertes, 146
Suprême de sole Philippe, 82
Suprême de turbot à la moëlle, 86
Suprême de volaille Paul Bocuse, 145
Suprême de volaille à la mangue, 143
Sweetbread:
   calves', with spinach, 135
   calves', steamed with truffles, vegetables and cream sauce, 136
   with soft boiled eggs and mushrooms, 74
   with terrine and chicken, 48
Sweetcorn, creamed, with pancakes, 167

Terrine:
   Covent Garden, 44
   de foie de canard, 49
   de hareng à l'aneth, 47
   de ris de veau et de volaille, 48
   de torteau à l'oseille, 111
Terrine:
   crabmeat, with sorrel sauce, 111
   duck liver, 49
   herring, with dill, 47
   with sweetbread and chicken, 48
   vegetable, 44
Timbale de brochet Palace, 102
Timbale de sole Eugène Käufeler, 83
Tomates concassées, 36
Tomatoes:
   chopped, 36
   with homemade ravioli and mushrooms, 55
   purée, with scallop mousseline, 57
   in Trianon de légumes, 166
   vinaigrette, 46
Tourte aux écrevisses, 53
Trianon de légumes, 166
Tronçon de turbot soufflé aux écrevisses, 87

Trout:
  fresh river, with chives, 81
  mousse Dorchester-style, with smoked
    salmon, 42
Truffles:
  with chicken liver parfait, 51
  sauce, 27
  with steamed calves' sweetbreads,
    vegetables and cream sauce, 131
Turbot:
  fillets, with marrow, 86
  fillets, with mustard sauce, 88
  fillets, with oysters and julienne of
    vegetables, 90
  goujons of, with saffron, 89
  soufflé, with crayfish, 87

Vanilla:
  cream, 179
  ice cream, 193
Veal:
  brown stock, 4
  cutlets, with stuffed morels, 131
  fillet, with cheese and green noodles, 128
  fillet, with goose liver, 134
  kidneys, in mustard sauce, 138
  kidneys, in red wine vinegar sauce, 137
  liver quenelles, with double consommé, 62
  medallions with oranges and lemons, 130

  mignons, in cream sauce and sorrel, 129
  strips, in cream sauce with mixed
    mushrooms, 133
  white stock, 2
  (see also Calves' liver; Calves' sweetbreads)
Vegetables(s):
  cold soup with basil, 61
  grilled, with baby chicken, 149
  julienne, with fillets of turbot, 90
  julienne, with scallop soup, 70
  three selected, 166
  terrine Covent Garden, 44
Venison:
  mignons, with parsley purée, 154
  sautéd medallions, with mushrooms in
    game sauce, 155
Vinaigrette (sauce):
  with fillets of red mullet, 99
  with French goose liver salad, 39
  with lobster salad, 37
  with oyster salad, 40
  tomato, 46

Walnut petits fours, 201
Western sauce, 25, 140
Wild duck:
  broth, 12
  fillets with juniper berry sauce, 162
Wild rice stuffing (for quails), 160